MacMath 9.0

John H. Hubbard
Beverly H. West

MacMath 9.0

A Dynamical Systems Software Package
for the Macintosh™

With 164 illustrations

Springer-Verlag

New York Berlin Heidelberg London Paris
Tokyo Hong Kong Barcelona Budapest

John H. Hubbard
Beverly H. West
Department of Mathematics
Cornell University
Ithaca, NY
USA

Mathematics Subject Classification: 34-00, 34A50, 34C05, 34C35

Cover illustration adapted from a printout generated by the PLANETS program of MacMath 9.0.

Library of Congress Cataloging-in-Publication Data
Hubbard, John H.
    MacMath : a dynamical systems software package for the Macintosh /
John H. Hubbard, Beverly H. West.
        p.   cm.
    Includes bibliographical references and index.
    ISBN 0-387-97416-4
    1. MacMath.   2. Differential equations—Data processing.
3. Differential equations, Partial—Data processing.   4. Macintosh
(Computer)—Programming.   I. West, Beverly Henderson, 1939–   .
II. Title.
QA371.H773 1991
5153'3'028566869—dc20   91-34297

Printed on acid-free paper.

Previous versions of this software were published by J.H. Hubbard and B. H. West, Cornell University 1985.

Production managed by Howard Ratner; Manufacturing supervised by Robert Paella.
Photocomposed copy prepared from author's $\mathcal{A}_{\mathcal{M}}\mathcal{S}$-TEX file.
Printed and bound by R.R. Donnelley & Sons, Harrisonburg, VA.
Printed in the United States of America.

9 8 7 6 5 4 3 2 1

ISBN 0-387-97416-4 Springer-Verlag New York Berlin Heidelberg
ISBN 3-540-97416-4 Springer-Verlag Berlin Heidelberg New York

Preface

MacMath is a scientific toolkit for the Macintosh™ computer developed by John H. Hubbard and Beverly H. West, consisting of twelve graphics programs. It supports mathematical computation and experimentation in dynamical systems, both for differential equations and for iteration. The **MacMath** package was designed to accompany the textbook *Differential Equations: A Dynamical Systems Approach*, also by J. H. Hubbard and B. H. West (Part I, *One Dimensional Equations*, 1990; Part II, *Higher Dimensional Systems*, 1991; Springer-Verlag).

We have developed this text and software for a junior-senior level course in Applicable Mathematics at Cornell University, in order to take advantage of the new qualitative and geometric insights made possible by the advent of excellent and easily accessible graphics. Our primary reasons are two:

1. *A picture is worth a thousand words.* Graphics are far more than just a luxury — the human brain is made to process *visual* information; more information can be assimilated in a few seconds of looking at a graphics output than in months of analyzing a tabulated computer printout, perhaps a centimeter thick, carrying the same numerical information.

2. *From qualitative analysis we can obtain excellent quantitative information.* Sometimes this idea applies directly to numerical results, as in finding a vertical asymptote to as many decimal places as desired. Other times the pictures provide a guide to what can (or cannot) be proved. For instance, for $x' = x^2 - t$ we can show that most solutions asymptotically approach $x = -\sqrt{t}$; this is a far more quantitative statement than just that these solutions go off to negative infinity — it tells exactly *how* they go off.

A further goal of the text is to bring to the study of continuous *differential equations* valuable insights from the theory of *iteration* by finite steps. Iteration is in fact what digital computers do, and the numerical approximations to solutions of differential equations are simply iterations. *Difference equations*, which are the finite analogs of differential equations, are also iterations.

Dynamical systems in general, which are often differential equations or iterations in particular, are the main tool with which scientists make mathematical models of real systems. As such they have a central role in connecting the power of mathematics with a description of the world. We shall give a brief overview of why this is so and how the **MacMath** programs help.

Ithaca, New York

John H. Hubbard
Beverly H. West

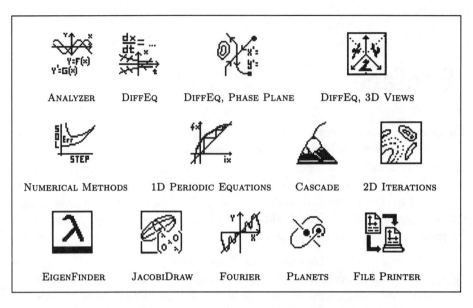

ANALYZER　　DIFFEQ　　DIFFEQ, PHASE PLANE　　DIFFEQ, 3D VIEWS

NUMERICAL METHODS　　1D PERIODIC EQUATIONS　　CASCADE　　2D ITERATIONS

EIGENFINDER　　JACOBIDRAW　　FOURIER　　PLANETS　　FILE PRINTER

Documentation by Beverly West, with Bjørn Felsager and John Hubbard.

Manuscript preparation by Katrina Thomas and Graeme Bailey.

Contributions from Maria Korolov, Heather Park, Chris Pelkie, David Walend, and all the programmers:

Yelena Baranova	ANALYZER, SYSTEMS(x, y), FOURIER, NUMERICAL METHODS, ITERATION, 1D AND 2D PERIODIC EQUATIONS
Fassil Bekele	SYSTEMS(x, y), PLANETS
Daniel Brown	EIGENFINDER
Marc Christensen	2D ITERATIONS, ANALYZER, upgrade of all programs
Robert Farrell	DIFFEQ, parser for all programs
Ben Hinkle	SYSTEMS 3D, PLANETS, upgrade of all programs
Trey Jones	PLANETS, CASCADE, upgrade of all programs
Bobbie Meshoyrer	CASCADE, ANALYZER
Peter Sisson	EIGENFINDER, JACOBIDRAW

Note: SYSTEMS(x, y) has become DIFFEQ, PHASE PLANE. SYSTEMS(x, y, t), SYSTEMS(x, y, z), SYSTEMS 3D, and 2D PERIODIC EQUATIONS are all precursors of DIFFEQ, 3D VIEWS.

Contents

Preface   v

The Mathematics

  1   Dynamical Systems   1
  2   Differential Equations   5
  3   Iteration   19

The Programs

  4   Quick Synopsis of Programs   27
  5   General Overview of Program Operations   31
  6   Analyzer   39
  7   DiffEq   47
  8   Numerical Methods   53
  9   DiffEq, Phase Plane   59
10   DiffEq, 3D Views   67
11   1D Periodic Equations   77
12   Cascade   81
13   2D Iterations   87
14   EigenFinder   95
15   JacobiDraw   101
16   Fourier   107
17   Planets   111

The Mathematics Revisited — Technical Reference

18   Linear Dynamical Systems   121
19   Bifurcations   131
20   Numerical Approximation   141
21   Troubleshooting   149

Index   155

1

Dynamical Systems

A *dynamical system* is a mathematical way of describing a system that *changes*. The basic observation of dynamical systems is that *the forces are simpler than the motions*. The classic example is Newton's description of motions of bodies under gravity. The forces are extremely simple: bodies attract with a force proportional to the product of their masses and inversely proportional to the square of the distance separating them. Yet the motions caused by these forces are extremely complex, resulting, for instance, in the braided rings of Saturn.

Differential equations and *iteration* are two approaches, continuous versus discrete, to dynamical systems. They use, respectively, differential and difference equations to describe the "forces", or directions in which a system is being pushed, given any initial state. A solution to a differential or difference equation describes the "motions" or actual path followed by an "object".

"Motions" sometimes refer to concrete "objects", under the influence of physical forces.

Example 1.1. (*Differential Equation*) The oscillation of a mass on a spring is described by setting the force according to Newton's Law equal to the force due to the action of the spring:

$$m\frac{d^2x}{dt^2} = -kx.$$

The solution $x = u(t)$ to this differential equation tells, for an initial position $u(0)$ and velocity $u'(0)$, exactly how x, the vertical distance from equilibrium, will change over time. The computer programs can show the graph of x versus t for any given initial conditions.

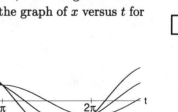

Solutions $x = u(t)$ for $\dfrac{d^2x}{dt^2} = -x$ (i.e., for the case where $k = m$).

In this example the differential equation may also be solved analytically, by hand, to give $x = A\cos(\sqrt{k/m}\,t + \phi)$, which indeed matches the solutions graphed. The MacMath programs make these algebraic calculations unnecessary.

Alternatively, the concepts of "force", "motion" and "object following a path" may be much more abstract, as in ecology where the "object" may be a vector list of various populations $(N_1, N_2, \ldots, N_n)$, for which we can write equations of the form

$$\frac{dN_j}{dt} = (\text{birthrate} - \text{deathrate})\, N_j.$$

In this equation, birth and death rates can themselves involve N_j or additional variables N_k (for $k \neq j$), in order to express the effects of such phenomena as crowding, predation, or competition.

Example 1.2. (*System of Differential Equations*)   The rates of change for populations of a single predator (foxes) and a single prey (rabbits) in an isolated environment can be expressed under a classic Lotka-Volterra model according to how frequently meetings between rabbits and foxes result in death for the rabbit and food for the fox.

$$\frac{dR}{dt} = (b_r - c_r F)R \quad \text{and} \quad \frac{dF}{dt} = (c_f R - d_f)F \,,$$

where R is the rabbit population, F the fox population, $d_r = c_r F$, the death rate of rabbits (depending on the number of foxes), and $b_f = c_f R$, the birth rate of foxes (depending on the number of rabbits).

The equation's solutions, $R = u(t)$ and $F = v(t)$, are observed to follow a cyclic pattern, one out of phase with the other, as shown in the following computer drawings, first for a single solution,

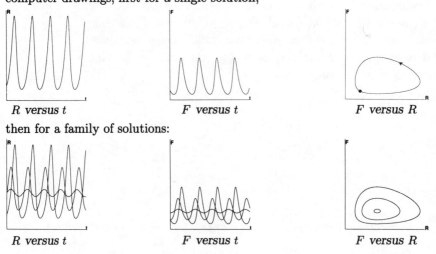

R versus t F versus t F versus R

then for a family of solutions:

R versus t F versus t F versus R

The right-most graph of Example 1.2, F versus R, is particularly valuable, and is called the *phase plane*. It is the one graph where t is not visible (except as the direction of the arrowhead), but it shows in a single picture the direct relation between the two populations. As the fox population increases from the initial point, the rabbit population decreases ... until there are few enough rabbits to bring down the fox population ... until there are few enough foxes that the rabbit population can begin to recover ... and so on.

A population problem could be alternatively stated as a *difference equation* with discrete, rather than continuous, time intervals. For instance, for a population $N(t)$, the population h time units later would follow

$$N(t + h) = N(t) + h \,(\text{birthrate} - \text{deathrate})\, N(t)$$
$$= [\, 1 + h \,(\text{birthrate} - \text{deathrate})\,]\, N(t).$$

Example 1.3. (*Difference Equation*) Consider fox and rabbit populations as in Example 1.2, but build a model based on measuring the populations at intervals of h time units. Then

$$R(t + h) \;=\; [\, 1 + h \,(b_r - c_r\, F(t)\,)\,]\, R(t)\ ,$$
$$F(t + h) \;=\; [\, 1 + h \,(c_f\, R(t) - d_f)\,]\, F(t)\ ,$$

where F is the predator population, R is the prey population, and h the time interval between measurements.

A difference equation like this will be handled by *iteration*, the process of repeating a procedure again and again, using the output of each step as the input for the next step.

This computer picture is of the phase plane F versus R (the graph of the dependent variables alone) for a particular stepsize ($h = 0.1$, here), starting at P when $t = 0$. This is now one cycle, which would close if h were smaller.

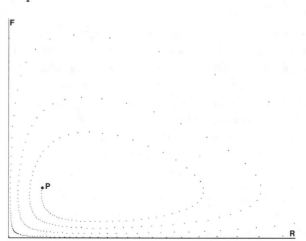

Phase plane for iteration of predator prey difference equation
$$F(t_{i+1}) \;=\; [\, 1 + h \,(1 - R(t_i)\,)\,]\, F(t_i)\ ,$$
$$R(t_{i+1}) \;=\; [\, 1 + h \,(0.5\, F(t_i) - 1)\,]\, R(t_i)\ .$$

A typical iteration behavior is shown in the right-hand picture of Example 1.3: each cycle slightly offsets its points.

Both differential equations and iteration of difference equations are commonly used to model real world situations, and as we have just shown, sometimes either might be applied to the same situation.

At first glance it might seem that iteration would be simpler, particularly since difference equations avoid the calculus of derivatives. It is conceptually easy to set up difference equations, and computers can make short work of computing a great many steps. But it is not easy to predict what kinds of motions will result from iterating different functions. They do *not* always behave as nicely as the nearly cyclic Example 1.3. In fact, far less is known mathematically about the behavior of difference equations under iteration, particularly in the case of more than one dependent variable, than about the behavior of differential equations, which themselves are understood only in the very simplest cases.

Differential equations has long been a field in which a mathematician could spend a lifetime. The only large class of differential equations that are well understood are the *linear* ones (like Example 1.1, where the variables and their derivatives occur only in first degree terms), which come up in real world models as approximations, often highly unreliable approximations, to the actual solutions. The *nonlinear* equations involve second or higher degree terms like x^2, y^2, xy, or nonlinear functions like trigonometric, exponential, rational, – e.g., $\sin x$, e^x, $\dfrac{t+x}{t-x}$. Nonlinear equations are far more of a challenge because far less is known about them. (Example 2 is nonlinear because it contains the second degree terms FR.)

The advent of easily accessible computer graphics has begun a revolution in the ways in which we can study nonlinear differential equations, a revolution that is particularly helpful to the student or scientist seeking to understand or apply the mathematics. Computer graphics has also made iteration one of the hottest research topics in mathematics today. An unusual aspect of this forefront research, either in nonlinear differential equations or in iteration, is that it is accessible to the mathematical neophyte. No fancy background in advanced mathematics is necessary to experiment with these processes; students as well as instructors can explore and get excited about new examples and applications.

In studying either differential equations or iteration there is much to be gained at an early stage by using these graphics programs. We will discuss separately and in greater detail the mathematics of these two types of dynamical systems, first with differential equations, then with iteration.

2

Differential Equations

Introductory Examples 1.1 and 1.2 illustrate *differential equations*, with variables that can vary continuously. Historically differential equations have received far more attention than finite difference equations or iteration.

One focus was on those differential equations that could be solved explicitly by *analytic techniques* such as direct integration and separation of variables, or by applying methods specific to linear equations, exact equations, and various other special types. Details of these solution techniques are left to any text on differential equations; they are not necessary for using and understanding the three **MacMath** graphics programs for differential equations: DIFFEQ, DIFFEQ, PHASE PLANE, and DIFFEQ, 3D VIEWS. (DIFFEQ is pronounced in three syllables: Diff - Eee - QUE.)

The fact of overriding importance is that differential equations in general do *not* lend themselves to these specialized methods. Although traditional courses in differential equations tend to be built about the equations that *are* solvable analytically, the raw equations desired for real world modeling often do not fall into those neat categories.

However, now we have a good way to deal with equations whether or not they can be solved explicitly. If the equations can be stated as functions in one of the following forms:

one-dimensional　　　　　*two-dimensional*　　　　　*three-dimensional*

$$\frac{dx}{dt} = f(t, x)$$

$$\frac{dx}{dt} = f(x, y)$$
$$\frac{dy}{dt} = g(x, y)$$

$$\frac{dx}{dt} = f(t, x, y)$$
$$\frac{dy}{dt} = g(t, x, y)$$

$$\frac{dx}{dt} = f(x, y, z)$$
$$\frac{dy}{dt} = g(x, y, z)$$
$$\frac{dz}{dt} = h(x, y, z)$$

DIFFEQ　　　　　DIFFEQ,　　　　　DIFFEQ, 3D VIEWS
　　　　　PHASE PLANE

then they can be entered in the indicated **MacMath** program. Higher order equations involving second and third derivatives can be rewritten to fit the above formats. The number of *dimensions* refers to the number of dependent variables. The **MacMath** programs *draw* the solutions (automatically, using standard *numerical methods*, to be discussed later) without any further user calculation.

In this section we shall take a qualitative approach to explain all this, starting with the simplest case.

The One-Dimensional Case

The DIFFEQ equation $\dfrac{dx}{dt} = f(t, x)$ describes a *slope field* in the tx-plane.

For any particular point (t, x) the equation tells exactly the slope of the solution through that point. The program draws the slope field by plotting, at the points of some grid, little line segments with the slope as given by the differential equation.

Example 2.1a. (*First Order Differential Equation*)

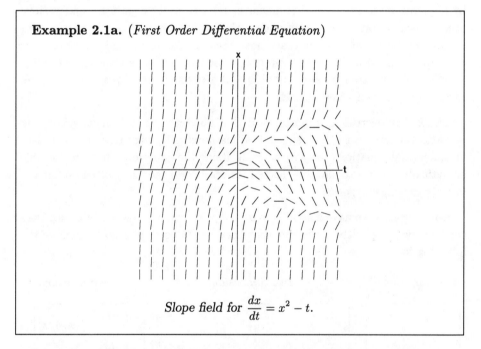

Slope field for $\dfrac{dx}{dt} = x^2 - t$.

A *solution* $x(t)$ of the differential equation is a function of t, which can be most easily imagined as a graph whose slope at every point (t, x) is $f(t, x)$.

If a *point* (t_0, x_0) is chosen by the cursor, the program will draw an *approximate solution* through that point. The point (t_0, x_0) is called the initial condition for that solution. The general idea of the approximate solution is that the computer calculates the slope at the initial condition and takes one step; then it calculates the new slope at that point and takes another step; then it repeats the process until it reaches the edge of the window. At that point it goes back to the initial condition and does the same thing in the opposite direction, going backwards along t.

Example 2.1b.

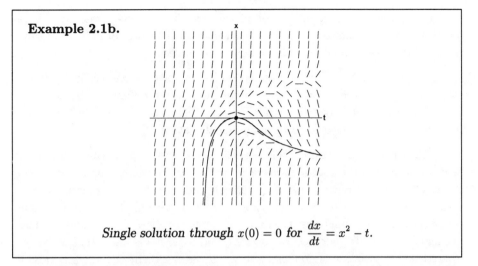

Single solution through $x(0) = 0$ for $\dfrac{dx}{dt} = x^2 - t$.

At the far right of this graph for Example 2.1b, the slope field changes rapidly near the solution drawn, but it has been calculated carefully with a stepsize of less than one pixel, so at every point graphed it indeed has the proper slope, as if a slope mark were centered on that point. The approximate solution travels "with the flow" through the slope field.

An approximate solution made in this way can be as accurate as you want. Choosing a smaller *stepsize* is one way (although it will take more time); choosing a more sophisticated *method* is another way (accounting for how the slope varies while one step is being taken, which will also take more time). The default stepsize and method give a good picture quickly for most equations you might enter.

You can choose another initial condition and then another until your screen has as many solutions displayed as you want.

Example 2.1c.

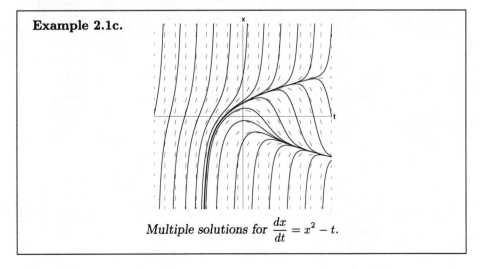

Multiple solutions for $\dfrac{dx}{dt} = x^2 - t$.

You now have a global picture of all the solutions at once, which enables a qualitative analysis quite unavailable from numerical listings of individual solutions, all that was available before computer graphics.

Furthermore, notice that the entire procedure of drawing an approximate solution uses only the *slope*, as given explicitly by the differential equation; it never makes any reference to an explicit analytic solution. The graphics program totally bypasses the need for such analytic calculation.

For the case of this example, this is particularly fortunate, because $x' = x^2 - t$ does not fit any of the special situations for analytic solutions; moreover, it can actually be proven (with very advanced mathematics from differential Galois theory) that for this particular equation there is no formula for the solutions in terms of elementary functions (the functions we normally write, like polynomials, rational functions, trigonometric functions, and other transcendental functions). Nevertheless the solutions do exist, and we are seeing them in these pictures.

Caution: You must always *think* about whether your picture is accurate. Your choice of stepsize must be small enough that solutions do not cross, in general. Default settings of graph coordinates, method, and stepsize usually, but not always, suffice. Discussion is provided in Section 21, **Troubleshooting**, of some of the factors that can produce a false picture, as well as examples of incorrect pictures; some are easily recognized as incorrect, while others are not. You should always verify that what you are seeing makes sense for your problem.

Raising the Number of Dimensions

Similar pictures to those in DIFFEQ can be drawn (using the programs DIFFEQ, PHASE PLANE, and DIFFEQ, 3D VIEWS) for a differential equation of *higher order* or with *more variables*, as discussed in our original examples. The overriding principle for changing a higher order equation in x into a system is to set $dx/dt = y$. If a higher degree is necessary, set $dy/dt = z$ and continue.

Example 2.2a.   The second order differential equation of Example 1.1 can be written as a system of two first order equations. If you introduce another variable $y = \dfrac{dx}{dt}$, then $\dfrac{d^2x}{dt^2} = \dfrac{dy}{dt}$, so

$$m\frac{d^2x}{dt^2} = -kx \quad \text{can be rewritten as} \quad \begin{cases} \dfrac{dx}{dt} = y, \\ \dfrac{dy}{dt} = -\dfrac{k}{m}x, \end{cases}$$

which is a system of two first order equations (such as we have already dealt with in Example 1.2).

In fact, any higher order differential equation can be rewritten as a system of first order equations, and this is what we must do in order to enter them in the **MacMath** programs.

The Two-Dimensional Case, Autonomous Equations

A two-dimensional system of differential equations for dx/dt and dy/dt may be *autonomous*, if there is no explicit dependence on t, or *nonautonomous*, if t appears in the functions for dx/dt and dy/dt.

An autonomous system describes a vector field in the xy-plane, the *phase plane*, consisting only of the dependent variables. Through any given point (x_0, y_0), the program DIFFEQ, PHASE PLANE will draw a *trajectory*, which is the xy-path determined parametrically by the solutions $x = u(t)$ and $y = v(t)$. For any particular point (x_0, y_0) the equations tell exactly the slope of the trajectory through that point by

$$\frac{dy}{dx} = \frac{dy/dt}{dx/dt} \; .$$

Example 2.2b. The simplest special case of Example 1.1, with $k = m = 1$, is

$$\frac{d^2x}{dt^2} = -x, \quad \text{which is equivalent to} \quad \begin{cases} \dfrac{dx}{dt} = y \; , \\ \dfrac{dy}{dt} = -x. \end{cases}$$

The phase plane trajectories turn out to be circles.

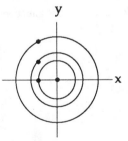

Phase plane trajectories for the three solutions shown in Example 1.1. Initial conditions are

$$\begin{aligned} x_0 &= u(0) = -1 \; , \\ y_0 &= u'(0) = 0, 1, 2 \; . \end{aligned}$$

The program DiffEq, Phase Plane gives you only trajectories in the xy-phase plane; this program does not show the individual solutions $x = u(t)$ and $y = v(t)$. You will in fact be able later to obtain xt and yt graphs from a system of differential equations, using extra capabilities of DiffEq, 3D Views.

The phase plane, however, shows how x and y interact; it is an extremely important picture. In particular, the phase plane gives crucial information about the behavior of trajectories near all possible *equilibria*. Also, for an autonomous system of differential equations, the trajectories normally will not meet or cross each other (except at equilibria).

An *equilibrium*, or a *singularity*, is a point where the derivative of each variable is zero; for Example 2.2b, the equilibrium is at $(0,0)$. An equilibrium may be either *stable* or *unstable*, according to whether nearby trajectories approach or leave that point; the center of Example 2.2b is stable in the physical sense, but neither attracting nor repelling.

If a system is *linear*, with *constant coefficients*, as in the last examples, then a great deal is known about the behavior of the trajectories. In fact, tradition-ally the only big success at finding analytic solutions was in dealing with linear equations with constant coefficients.

Nonlinear systems turn out not to be so different as you might think, now that phase plane pictures are so readily obtained. The phase plane allows us to see what happens to trajectories, especially near singularities, and to see that there the nonlinear equations behave exactly as the linear ones. So phase plane analysis for linear equations even serves for nonlinear ones.

Linear Equations With Constant Coefficients

In a two-dimensional system of differential equations, there are essentially four types of equilibria, named for the typical pictures of phase plane trajectories near them:

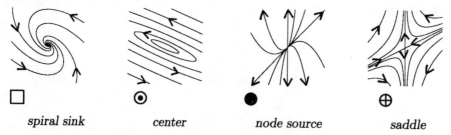

| □ | ⊙ | ● | ⊕ |
| spiral sink | center | node source | saddle |

Sources (arrows point out) or *sinks* (arrows point in) are further subdivided into "spirals" and "nodes". A *saddle* has some arrows pointing out, some point-ing in, as shown.

The spirals and centers correspond to solutions with trigonometric factors in sine and cosine functions (e.g., $e^{-t}\sin t$); these are the cases where the individual solutions will represent periodic motion (resonant or damped in the cases of sources and sinks, respectively), as we saw in Examples 1.1 and 2.2 and will elaborate when we get to DIFFEQ, 3D VIEWS.

The nodes and saddles represent the possible combinations of two principal vector directions, each of which can represent stable equilibrium (inward pointing) or unstable equilibrium (outward pointing).

The program DIFFEQ, PHASE PLANE will locate and identify singularities. It does so, one at a time, with a two variable Newton's Method, finding where $dx/dt = 0$ and $dy/dt = 0$ simultaneously, given an initial guess with the cursor. You will usually want to examine some sample trajectories in order to guess where there will be a singularity, then ask for it with an initial guess close by. A linear system will have a single singularity; a nonlinear system may have more, as in the following:

Example 2.3.
$$x' = y ,$$
$$y' = 1 - x^2 + y .$$

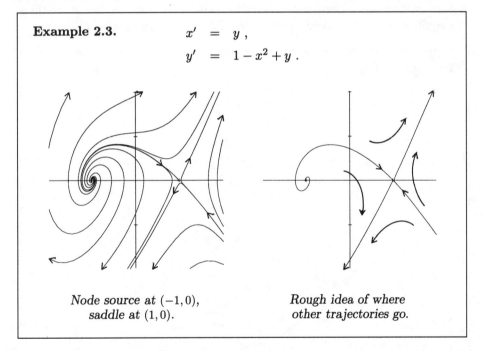

Node source at $(-1, 0)$,
saddle at $(1, 0)$.

Rough idea of where
other trajectories go.

In the case of a saddle, the program also draws the *separatrices*, that is, two forward and two backward trajectories from the singularity. These unique trajectories separate behaviors over the entire phase plane. Once you know where the separatrices go, you will be able to predict where any trajectory will go, as in the right-hand picture of Example 2.3.

A *linear* system of two first order differential equations (alternatively, a single second order equation) will exhibit a single equilibrium or singularity, showing one of the six behaviors (or a degenerate case, corresponding to double and/or zero eigenvalues). Some degenerate possibilities are shown on the next page.

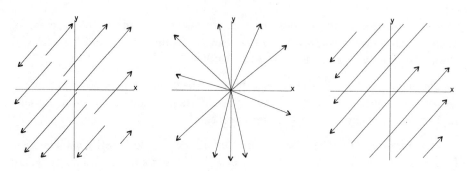

Possible degenerate equilibria.

Nonlinear Equations

A *nonlinear* system of two first order differential equations can have more than one equilibrium or singularity, and may exhibit a very complicated phase plane.

Example 2.4.

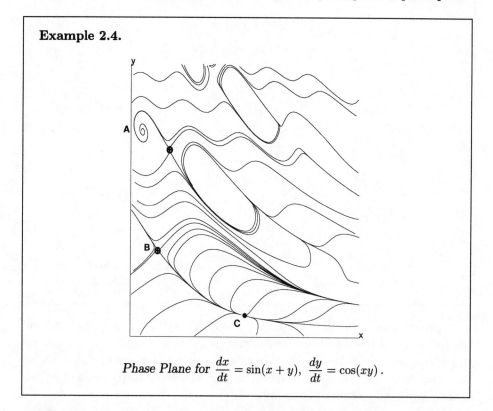

Phase Plane for $\dfrac{dx}{dt} = \sin(x + y),\ \dfrac{dy}{dt} = \cos(xy)$.

The option in DIFFEQ, PHASE PLANE to locate singularities will again do so, one at a time. Note that at every singularity or equilibrium, the nonlinear phase plane trajectories behave exactly like a linear system, as you will see if you blow up (zoom into) the nonlinear phase plane sufficiently about any equilibrium.

Blowup near
singularity A

Blowup near
singularity B

Blowup near
singularity C

There is only one other phase plane behavior a nonlinear system can exhibit – a *limit cycle*, which can be attracting or repelling.

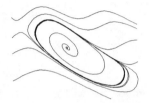

Limit Cycle.

For a nonlinear system, a good approximation to a solution can be made, by the process of *linearization*, near the singularity. The linearization formulas are given in Example 18.1 in Section 18, **Linear Dynamical Systems**; here we just let the pictures speak for themselves.

Example 2.5. (*Linearization of a System of Differential Equations*)

Consider another system of nonlinear ordinary differential equations:

$$x' = y(x+1),$$
$$y' = (3-y)x.$$

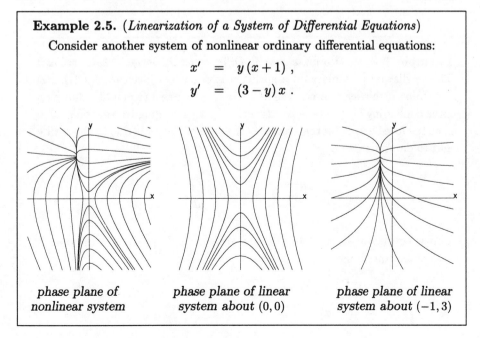

phase plane of
nonlinear system

phase plane of linear
system about $(0,0)$

phase plane of linear
system about $(-1,3)$

The Two-Dimensional Case, Nonautonomous Equations

The program DIFFEQ, 3D VIEWS is an extension of DIFFEQ, PHASE PLANE, so we shall rely heavily on the preceding discussion of two-dimensional systems in the sense of not redefining all the terms. The program DIFFEQ, 3D VIEWS allows us to see one more dimension, and there are two ways in which we might want to do this.

The first is to simply use the third dimension to study the two-dimensional system

$$\frac{dx}{dt} = f(t, x, y) ,$$

$$\frac{dy}{dt} = g(t, x, y) .$$

If this system is autonomous we will get more information than from the phase plane alone; if the system is nonautonomous, the phase plane portrait is not meaningful, but the new options will permit other analysis. Now we can include t in the graphs, so there are several possible pictures: a three-dimensional figure in txy-space, and three two-dimensional figures in the tx-, ty-, and xy-planes. In each of these views an *approximate solution* can be drawn from an initial condition in the same general manner as before; again no analytic solution is necessary.

Example 2.6. (*Two-dimensional Differential Equation, Autonomous*) The oscillation of a mass on a spring was described in Examples 1.1 and 2.2. If for such a system we take $m = 1$ and $k = 1$ and then add a damping force depending on the velocity, dx/dt, we get, according to Newton's Law, that the force acting on the system is the sum of the force due to the spring and to damping:

$$\frac{d^2 x}{dt^2} = -x - 0.3\,\frac{dx}{dt} .$$

This is equivalent to the following two-dimensional system of autonomous first order equations:

$$\frac{dx}{dt} = y , \qquad \frac{dy}{dt} = -x - 0.3\,y .$$

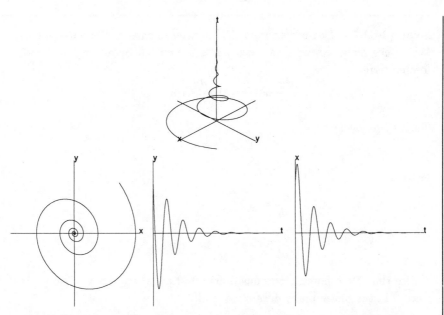

Simultaneous graphs for a single solution to a spring equation, like
Example 1.1, with a damping term added: $x'' + 0.3x' + x = 0$.

Adding another solution gives the following set of pictures, illustrating the
fact that only in the phase plane do you get a picture where the trajectories
do not cross.

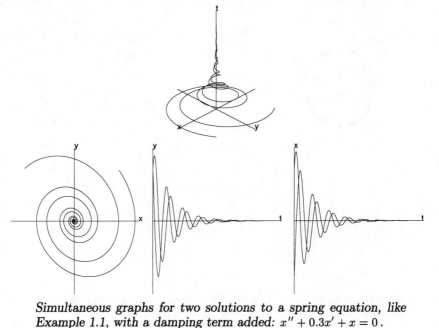

Simultaneous graphs for two solutions to a spring equation, like
Example 1.1, with a damping term added: $x'' + 0.3x' + x = 0$.

Example 2.7. (*Two-dimensional Differential Equation, Nonautonomous*)
We'll once more extend Examples 1.1, 2.2, and 2.6 by adding a periodic
forcing term:

$$\frac{d^2x}{dt^2} = -x - 0.3\frac{dx}{dt} + \sin t \ .$$

This is equivalent to

$$x'' + 0.3x' + x = \sin t$$

or to

$$\frac{dx}{dt} = y \ ,$$

$$\frac{dy}{dt} = -x - 0.3y + \sin t \ .$$

Notice that for a nonautonomous differential equation, even this one trajectory in the phase plane *does* cross itself.

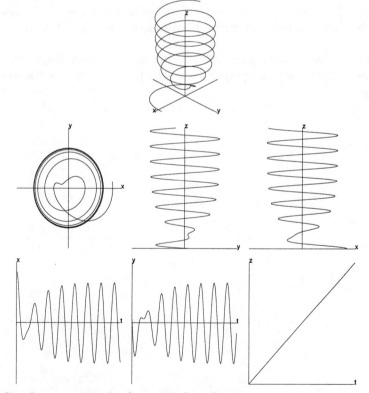

*Simultaneous graphs for a single solution to a nonautonomous
spring equation with forcing term:* $x'' + 0.3x' + x = \sin t$.

The Three-Dimensional Case

The second instance in which a third dimension aids in visualizing a system of differential equations is when there is a third dependent variable. The program DIFFEQ, 3D VIEWS will accept an autonomous three-dimensional system, that is, with no explicit dependence on t:

$$\frac{dx}{dt} = f(x,y,z) , \qquad \frac{dy}{dt} = g(x,y,z) , \qquad \frac{dz}{dt} = h(x,y,z) .$$

In such an autonomous three-dimensional system, the critical graph that relates x, y, and z is a three-dimensional xyz-phase space, and there are now six possible two-dimensional planar pictures of the same trajectory: tx, ty, tz, xy, xz, yz.

Example 2.8. (*Three-dimensional Differential Equation*)

Here are simultaneous graphs for a single trajectory of the system

$$\frac{dx}{dt} = y ,$$

$$\frac{dy}{dt} = -x ,$$

$$\frac{dz}{dt} = \frac{1}{(|z| + 0.1)} .$$

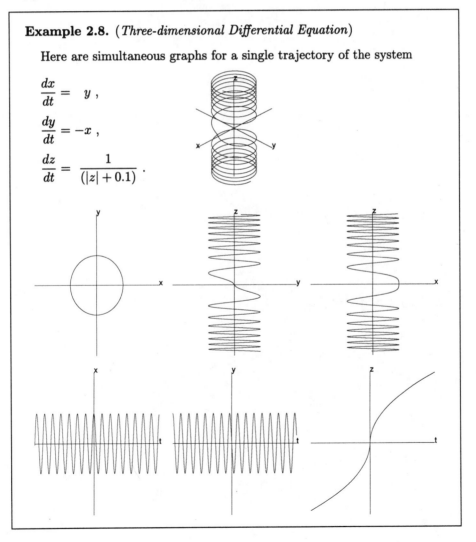

3

Iteration

Iteration is the process of repeating the same procedure over and over, using *output of one step as input for the next.* We start with a *function* $f(x)$ and a *seed* x_0, then set

$$
\begin{aligned}
x_1 &= f(x_0) \\
x_2 &= f(x_1) &= f(f(x_0)) &= f^{\circ 2}(x_0) \\
x_3 &= f(x_2) &= f(f(f(x_0))) &= f^{\circ 3}(x_0) \\
&\vdots
\end{aligned}
$$

The sequence $x_0, x_1, x_2, x_3, \ldots$ is called the orbit of x_0 under f. What happens to the orbit when you iterate depends both on the function and on the seed.

Example 3.1a. (*Iteration*)   Consider the simple squaring function, $f(x) = x^2$. Iterating for different seeds gives the following results:

seed	$f(x) = x^2$	observations
$x_0 = 2$	$2, 4, 16, 256, \ldots \to \infty$	*unbounded* orbit
$x_0 = 1/2$	$1/2, 1/4, 1/16, 1/256, \ldots \to 0$	*bounded* orbit, attracted by 0
$x_0 = 1$	$1, 1, 1, 1, \ldots \to 1$	*bounded* orbit, which is a *fixed point*, because $f(x) = x$.

The three different seeds in Example 3.1 show three different orbit behaviors. The big question is how to predict what will happen for a particular seed.

The One-Dimensional Case

The orbit of x under iteration of f may exhibit various behaviors. For a particular function and a particular seed, a key to predicting what will happen lies in the *graphical picture* of iteration. The program ANALYZER will do this graphical iteration quickly and accurately. The idea is to graph $f(x)$ and the diagonal line $y = x$, and to choose an x_0 on the x-axis. Then

(1) Draw a vertical line to the curve (thus calculating the output $f(x_0)$).
(2) Go from that point horizontally to the diagonal line $y = x$ (thus converting output $f(x_0)$ to input x_1).

Repeat these two steps by moving vertically from the new point x_1 on the diagonal, to the curve $f(x_1)$ to get x_2, and continue in this fashion.

Example 3.1b. (*Graphical Iteration*)   Consider again $f(x) = x^2$.

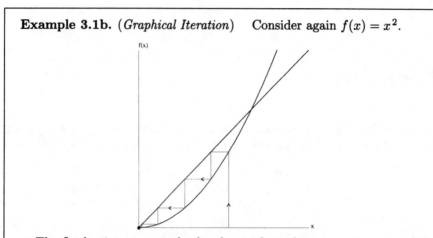

The *fixed points* are exactly the places where the curve crosses the diagonal, because there $f(x) = x$. A fixed point may be *attracting* (as in the above illustration), or *repelling* (as illustrated below by the rightmost and leftmost orbits).

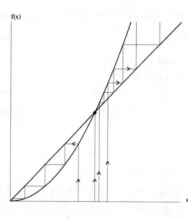

Zero is a fixed point, because $0^2 = 0$; 1 is a fixed point, because $1^2 = 1$.

Seeds between 0 and 1 have orbits attracted to 0 and repelled by 1.

Seeds greater than 1 have unbounded orbits, also repelled by 1.

What determines whether a fixed point is attracting or repelling is the *slope* of $f(x)$ at the fixed point:

attracting fixed points have slope $|f'(x)| < 1$;

repelling fixed points have slope $|f'(x)| > 1$.

Furthermore,

if the slope $|f'(x)| = 1$, the fixed point is called *neutral* or *indifferent*, because anything can happen;

if the slope $f'(x) = 0$, the fixed point is called *superattracting*, because it attracts very fast.

Example 3.2. (*An Attracting Cycle*) Consider the iteration of $f(x) = x^2 - 1$.

seed	$f(x) = x^2 - 1$	observations.
$x_0 = 0$	$0, -1, 0, -1, 0, -1, \ldots$	the orbit is a cycle, period 2.
$x_0 = 1$	$1, 0, -1, 0, -1, 0, -1, \ldots$	the orbit is attracted to the same cycle.

The iteration graphs for both these seeds look the same from 0 on. Let's try something harder, like $x_0 = 1.5$ (displaying only the first four digits of each iterate):

$$x_1 = (1.5)^2 - 1 = 1.25$$
$$x_2 = (1.25)^2 - 1 = 0.5625$$
$$x_3 = (.5625)^2 - 1 = -0.6836$$
$$x_4 = = -0.5327$$
$$x_5 = = -0.7162$$
$$x_6 = = -0.4870$$
$$x_7 = = -0.7628$$
$$x_8 = = -0.4181$$
$$x_9 = = -0.8252$$
$$x_{10} = = -0.3191$$
$$x_{11} = = -0.8982$$
$$x_{12} = = -0.1932$$
$$x_{13} = = -0.9627$$
$$x_{14} = = -0.0733$$
$$x_{15} = = -0.9946$$
$$x_{16} = = -0.0107$$
$$x_{17} = = -0.9999$$
$$x_{18} = = -0.0002$$
$$x_{19} = = -0.9999$$
$$x_{20} = = -0.0000\ldots$$

You can see from both the numbers and the graph that the orbit gets closer and closer to the cycle $0, -1, 0, -1, 0, -1, \ldots$, illustrating that the cycle is an attracting one.

You can find the fixed points exactly by solving the equation $x^2 - 1 = x$ to get

$$x = \frac{1 \pm \sqrt{5}}{2} = 1.618\ldots \quad \text{or} \quad -0.618\ldots.$$

Both are repelling fixed points, so the iteration list does not detect them.

You should use ANALYZER to experiment with different functions and different seeds. These examples just hint at the incredibly complicated set of behaviors resulting from the process of iterating the simple functions of the form $x^2 + c$. With further study, and the program CASCADE, you can also investigate the *cascade of bifurcations* that explains the overall pattern of changing behaviors with changing values of the parameter c.

The Two-Dimensional Case

Iteration in two dimensions consists of enlarging the "output as input" idea to two variables, so we have

$$x_{n+1} = f(x_n, y_n),$$
$$y_{n+1} = g(x_n, y_n).$$

Example 3.3a. (*Iteration in Two Dimensions*)

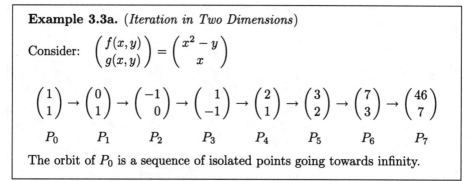

Consider: $\begin{pmatrix} f(x,y) \\ g(x,y) \end{pmatrix} = \begin{pmatrix} x^2 - y \\ x \end{pmatrix}$

$\begin{pmatrix} 1 \\ 1 \end{pmatrix} \rightarrow \begin{pmatrix} 0 \\ 1 \end{pmatrix} \rightarrow \begin{pmatrix} -1 \\ 0 \end{pmatrix} \rightarrow \begin{pmatrix} 1 \\ -1 \end{pmatrix} \rightarrow \begin{pmatrix} 2 \\ 1 \end{pmatrix} \rightarrow \begin{pmatrix} 3 \\ 2 \end{pmatrix} \rightarrow \begin{pmatrix} 7 \\ 3 \end{pmatrix} \rightarrow \begin{pmatrix} 46 \\ 7 \end{pmatrix}$

$\quad P_0 \qquad P_1 \qquad P_2 \qquad P_3 \qquad P_4 \qquad P_5 \qquad P_6 \qquad P_7$

The orbit of P_0 is a sequence of isolated points going towards infinity.

As in the one-dimensional iteration, different seeds lead to quite different orbits. But we need an entirely different kind of picture to represent iteration in two variables, since it takes a plane to represent a point (x, y).

Example 3.3b.

Iterating $\begin{pmatrix} f(x,y) \\ g(x,y) \end{pmatrix} = \begin{pmatrix} x^2 - y \\ x \end{pmatrix}$.

We will make pictures of several orbits. First is the one we computed in Example 3.3a,

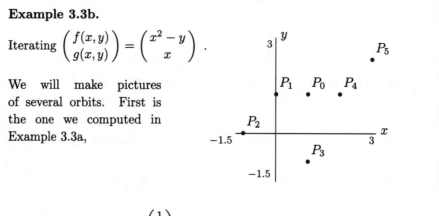

the orbit with seed $P_0 = \begin{pmatrix} 1 \\ 1 \end{pmatrix}$, with $P_6, P_7, \ldots$ going off to the upper right.

Consider another orbit with seed $P_0 = \begin{pmatrix} 1/2 \\ 1/4 \end{pmatrix}$:

$$\begin{pmatrix} 1/2 \\ 1/4 \end{pmatrix} \longrightarrow \begin{pmatrix} 0 \\ 1/2 \end{pmatrix} \longrightarrow \begin{pmatrix} -1/2 \\ 0 \end{pmatrix} \longrightarrow \begin{pmatrix} 1/4 \\ -1/2 \end{pmatrix} \longrightarrow \begin{pmatrix} 9/16 \\ 1/4 \end{pmatrix}$$

$$P_0 \qquad\qquad P_1 \qquad\qquad P_2 \qquad\qquad P_3 \qquad\qquad P_4$$

Note that P_4 is very close to P_0, but shifted slightly to the right.

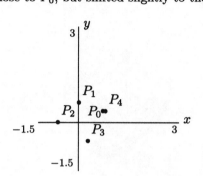

If we let this orbit continue, we see that it continues to cycle (almost) and shift, apparently filling in a closed curve! This orbit does not escape to infinity.

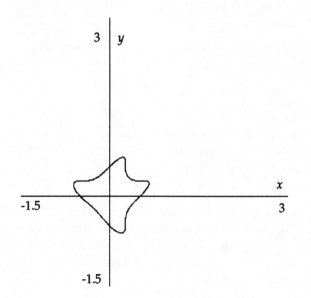

These two orbits are part of a large complicated picture which we show for several other orbits.

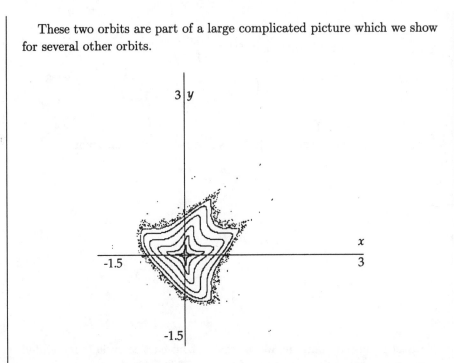

Each closed curve is an orbit for a different seed. The outermost "closed curve" is fuzzier, and the small dots outside it all belong to a single orbit which doesn't escape as fast as the big dot orbit of our first seed $P_0 = (1, 1)$.

Example 3.3 barely shows the beginning of the complexity of iteration in two dimensions. The default example

$$\begin{pmatrix} x \\ y \end{pmatrix} = \begin{pmatrix} x + 0.7y \\ y + 0.7 \left\{ (x + 0.7y) - (x + 0.7y)^3 / 25 \right\} \end{pmatrix}$$

for the 2D ITERATIONS program is illustrated several times in Section 13. There you can see and experiment with the fact that the separatrices, drawn in black (unstable) and dotted black (stable), can *cross* under iteration, unlike under differential equations.

We shall discuss some of the complicated behavior of iteration here below, with more in Section 13, **2D Iteration**, and Section 18, **Linear Dynamical Systems**. For a more complete discussion of iteration in two dimensions, see Chapter Thirteen in Hubbard and West, *Differential Equations: A Dynamical Systems Approach*, Volume II.

By far the best way to study iteration in two dimensions is to have a color monitor. A pretty good alternative for a black and white monitor is to have an Imagewriter II with multicolored ribbon; then the printouts will be in color even if the screen is not.

Behavior of Orbits Near Fixed Points

Under iteration, fixed points (and periodic points) come in several flavors; the coarsest classification is into sources, sinks, and saddles.

A fixed point $\mathbf{x}$ is a *sink* if all seeds chosen sufficiently near $\mathbf{x}$ have forward orbits tending to $\mathbf{x}$.

A fixed point $\mathbf{x}$ is a *source* if the backwards orbits of nearby points tend to it. An alternative explanation is that a fixed point $\mathbf{x}$ is a source if the mapping is invertible in a neighborhood of $\mathbf{x}$ and $\mathbf{x}$ is a sink for the inverse mapping.

So far this is very similar to the attracting and repelling fixed points of the one-dimensional iteration situation, but in two dimensions there is another possibility (in n dimensions there are $(n-1)$ new possibilities): *saddles*. These are fixed points $\mathbf{x}$ such that in some neighborhood U of $\mathbf{x}$ we have:

(1) the mapping is invertible in U;
(2) the seeds with forward iterates contained in U and attracted to $\mathbf{x}$ form a curve through $\mathbf{x}$, called the *stable separatrix* of $\mathbf{x}$;
(3) the seeds with backwards iterates contained in U and attracted to $\mathbf{x}$ also form a curve through $\mathbf{x}$, called the *unstable separatrix* of $\mathbf{x}$.

A simple example of a mapping having such a fixed point is given by

$$\begin{pmatrix} x \\ y \end{pmatrix} \longrightarrow \begin{pmatrix} 2x \\ \frac{1}{2}y \end{pmatrix} ;$$

the stable separatrix of the equilibrium at the origin $(0,0)$ is the y-axis, and the unstable separatrix the x-axis.

Locally, near the fixed points with which they are associated, separatrices for iterative systems are very similar to separatrices for differential equations in the plane. But their global behavior is wildly different. Nothing prevents the stable and unstable separatrix of a fixed point from intersecting, and when that happens, the sort of tangle you see (called a *homoclinic tangle*) on page 88 inevitably arises.

One can prove that in the presence of a homoclinic tangle there must be infinitely many periodic points, of arbitrarily high period, each with its own homoclinic tangle. So as soon as this occurs, the dynamics must be "infinitely complicated".

Iterating Linear Transformations

As in the case of differential equations, there is one class of mappings for which the iteration is well understood: *linear* mappings, those of the form

$$\begin{pmatrix} x \\ y \end{pmatrix} \longrightarrow \begin{pmatrix} ax + by \\ cx + dy \end{pmatrix} .$$

As in the case of linear mappings, these serve as local models for iterations of nonlinear mappings near fixed points and periodic cycles.

But behaviors of orbits under iteration are far less obvious in static pictures than for differential equations. Since discussion of them is best done with a little more mathematics, we postpone the details to Section 18, **Linear Dynamical Systems**, from a simple algebraic point of view.

Meanwhile, however, you can observe basic fixed point behavior dynamically by watching the orbit of a nearby point evolve step by step. If successive iterates get closer to the fixed point, for *any* seed near it, you probably have a sink. If some orbits get closer and others get further away, you probably have a saddle. Sometimes you'll see a pattern nearly cycling, but on closer inspection it turns out actually to be attracted or repelled by a fixed point. For instance, if you look back to Example 3.3b, you can see that the first picture shows that the fixed point $(0,0)$ seems to be a source, and that the second picture shows the start of a cyclic behavior.

One more complication of iteration orbits in two dimensions is the "flip" and "double" flip behavior, explained in Section 18. Here it suffices to note that an orbit may be continually reflected about an axis or the fixed point as successive iterates approach or go away from the fixed point.

Example 3.4.

$$\begin{pmatrix} x \\ y \end{pmatrix} \longrightarrow \begin{pmatrix} -0.9\,x \\ 0.8\,y \end{pmatrix}$$

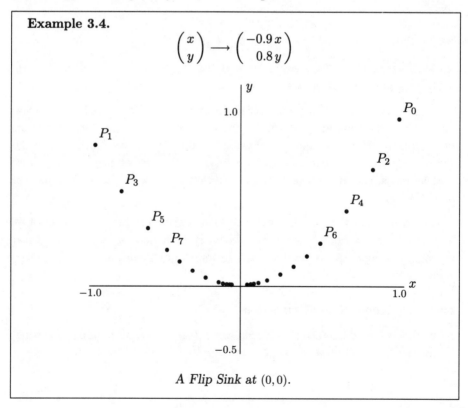

A Flip Sink at $(0,0)$.

4

Quick Synopsis of Programs

Analyzer

For a function of the form $y = f(x)$, this program will graph the function, find roots (either by a bisection method or by Newton's method), find maxima and minima (by analyzing the derivative), and numerically integrate the function with a choice of four methods. The program will also iterate a function graphically. Graphs of the function and its derivatives, or of different functions, can be overlaid. Analyzer is a very handy tool for dealing with awkward equations both numerically and graphically.

DiffEq

For a first order differential equation of the form $x' = f(t, x)$, this program displays a slope field and draws solutions in the tx-plane. The initial condition is chosen graphically with the cursor, and the coordinates of this starting point are displayed. The drawing of the solution proceeds first forward in time and then backward. The user has a choice of stepsize and method.

Numerical Methods

For a first order differential equation of the form $x' = f(t, x)$, this program will calculate a numerical solution, given initial values of t and x, a range of stepsizes, and a final value of t. In order to study what affects error, the program allows changing the number of bits accuracy, and it gives an option of rounding to nearest bit, always rounding up, or rounding down. It also calculates the error where possible, and the "order" p. (Each of the numerical methods corresponds to a different value of p.) Finally, the program graphs error versus stepsize.

DiffEq, Phase Plane

For an autonomous system of differential equations of the form

$$\frac{dx}{dt} = f(x, y), \qquad \frac{dy}{dt} = g(x, y)$$

this program displays the vector field in the xy-phase plane. It will also locate singularities (by Newton's method) and analyze them; for the saddles it draws the separatrices. Furthermore there is an option to locate either sink-source or saddle-node bifurcations for two-parameter families of equations.

DiffEq, 3D Views

For autonomous systems of differential equations of the form

$$\frac{dx}{dt} = f(x, y, z),$$

$$\frac{dy}{dt} = g(x, y, z),$$

$$\frac{dz}{dt} = h(x, y, z),$$

this program draws the three-dimensional phase space and relevant planar graphs; it also locates and analyzes singularities in xyz-space.

For nonautonomous systems of the form

$$\frac{dx}{dt} = f(t, x, y),$$

$$\frac{dy}{dt} = g(t, x, y),$$

the other option draws three-dimensional trajectories in txy-space. For either option, the program prints a numerical list of a trajectory, and rotates or "rocks" the 3D graph of the trajectories. Furthermore, for the case of a nonautonomous two-dimensional system where the functions f and g are *periodic* with respect to t, this program will graph trajectories in txy-space between two planes spaced for the entered period and give an xy-plane return map that plots the points for each iteration by one period.

1D Periodic Equations

This program studies differential equations of the form

$$\frac{dx}{dt} = f(t, x) \,,$$

where f is periodic with respect to t. The t interval setting represents one period. The program has two graph windows, one similar to DIFFEQ, and one which plots the period mapping.

Cascade

For two different functions of the form $f(x, c)$ this program displays changes in iteration behavior as the parameter c is varied. The result is the cascade of bifurcations that appears frequently throughout the study of "chaos". You can study the cascade either pictorially (by blowing up or by adjusting the number of marked and unmarked points) or analytically by iteration (of any n-th iterate).

2D Iterations

This program iterates functions of two variables of the form:

$$x_{n+1} = f(x_n, y_n), \qquad y_{n+1} = g(x_n, y_n).$$

It draws orbits, locates singular points, finds their period, analyzes them, and draws separatrices for saddles. Each orbit can be set to a different color.

EigenFinder

This program finds eigenvalues and eigenvectors for matrices up to size 12×12, to whatever precision you choose. Two methods are available: Jacobi's method, which is much faster but requires a symmetric matrix, and the QR algorithm, which is slower but will handle a nonsymmetric matrix.

JacobiDraw

This program geometrically demonstrates Jacobi's method of finding eigenvalues for a 3×3 matrix, by representing the matrix as a quadric surface (an ellipsoid, a hyperboloid, or a degenerate surface in the case of zero eigenvalues) and animating the rotational effects on the surface of the diagonalization of the matrix. That is, you can see the Spectral Theorem or Principal Axis Theorem in action. Each iteration of Jacobi's method corresponds to rotating the axes to eliminate the largest off-diagonal term; the process converges to a diagonal matrix of eigenvalues when the coordinate axes align with the quadric surface axes.

Fourier

For a given function $f(x)$, this program calculates Fourier approximations for a desired interval using the formula

$$f_k(x) = \sum_{n=0}^{k} a_n \cos nx + b_n \sin nx$$

for any order k and graphs the approximation. The function may be entered either by a formula in the usual way or by cursor in piecewise linear fashion.

Planets

This program animates the motion of up to ten bodies under the influence of either the gravitational or electrostatic forces they exert on one another. You can change the masses, positions, and velocities numerically. You can also change the positions or velocities graphically with the cursor. The program includes options for adding friction or for freezing a planet's position.

5

General Overview of Program Operation

It is assumed that the user is somewhat familiar with the operation of a Macintosh™, for example, starting a program or using a printer. The following information discusses the features which the **MacMath** programs have in common.

Warning: Problems may occur if these programs are used with Multifinder™, especially in printing and color applications.

To Enter a Function

Most programs in the **MacMath** package require either a function or a set of functions. You will be prompted with something like $y = $, or $dx/dt = $.

```
Please enter equation:
y= x 3 - 2*x 2 + 1

( OK )  (Cancel)  (Help)              (Quit program)
```

Often, there is a default provided and you can click on $\boxed{\text{OK}}$ to go with the default, or you can type in your own function. The first key you hit will replace the default equation. Proper syntax for entering functions is listed below. After you type in a function you can either change it using the $\boxed{\text{Delete}}$ key or the mouse, clicking on $\boxed{\text{OK}}$ to go on.

Valid Equation Elements	
+, -, *, /	Standard arithmetic operations
2, 3.7, .9, π	Numeric values
x	Variable
( )	Parentheses
ln()	Natural logarithm
exp()	Exponentiation of e
^	Exponentiation
abs()	Absolute value
sin,cos,tan, cot, atan,sinh,cosh	Trigonometric and hyperbolic trigonometric functions
sqrt	Square root
sgn	Sign of argument (1,0, or -1)
floor	Step function by truncation

(OK)

31

Note: When more than one function is needed, use the $\boxed{\text{Tab}}$ key or the mouse to advance to the text box for the next function. Whenever you are going to enter a function you can click $\boxed{\text{Help}}$ to get a list of the valid equation elements.

Symbols

Division: /   (slash)

Multiplication: *
(asterisk, $\boxed{\text{shift-8}}$)

Raising to a power: ^
(caret, $\boxed{\text{shift-6}}$)

Parentheses: ( )   (enclose
the argument of every function;
also used to avoid ambiguity)

Examples:

to mean $\dfrac{x+2}{x+6}$,

write   (x+2)/(x+6)

to mean $5x$,   write   5*x

to mean $x^2 + \sqrt[4]{\sin x}$,

write   x^2 + (sin(x))^0.25

to mean $\sin x$,
write   sin(x)

Note: Exponentiation, ^ , is slower (in general) than division or multiplication, so you may prefer $1/x$ to $x^{(-1)}$ and $x*x$ to x^2. The reason is that exponentiation tests the exponent to see if it is an integer at every evaluation.

Letters

Both lower and upper case letters are accepted, with no distinction made between lower case and upper case.

You can use π in a function by entering its symbol, π, by holding down the $\boxed{\text{Option}}$ key and typing $\boxed{\text{p}}$, or by typing in the word **pi**. The programs do not, however, accept the symbol **e** as the base of the natural logarithms. You must enter powers of e using the function **exp**. For example, e^x would be entered as **exp(x)**.

Note: A numeral '0' (zero) is different from an 'O' (oh), and a '1' (one) is different from an 'l' (lower-case 'L'). They look similar, but using the wrong one will cause the computer to give an error message.

Trigonometric and Other Functions

When entering an equation, you may use combinations of the following functions: **sin**, **cos**, **exp** (power of e), **ln** (natural logarithm), **abs** (absolute value), **tan**, **cot**, and **sqrt** (square root). The **MacMath** programs also support **atan** (arctangent) as well as the hyperbolic trigonometric functions **sinh** and **cosh**. Finally, the programs support the discontinuous functions **sgn** (sign of x) and **floor** (truncations of x to an integer value). Other functions, like secant and cosecant, are not supported, so you will have to enter them in terms of the ones that are. For example:

$$\sec(x) = \frac{1}{\cos(x)} \quad \text{and} \quad \csc(x) = \frac{1}{\sin(x)}.$$

Finally you should notice that in general the power functions like x^a (where a is not a natural number) are only defined for positive values of x. If, e.g., you want to use the cubic root function $x^{1/3}$ for all x it should therefore be entered as

$$\text{y = sgn(x) * abs(x) \^{} (1/3).}$$

To Select a Window

You must click (anywhere) in a window to activate it before you can click for another task in that window. When a window is active, it has a striped bar at the top.

To Change the Window Bounds

The programs provide several ways to change the scale along the axes in the drawing window. For example, if the numerical range of the axes is displayed on the screen, you can point the mouse to the selected values, click, and then edit them. If the ranges are in a separate box, or window, you might have to first click on the box in order to select it. You will have to click on $\boxed{\text{OK}}$ as well, for the new values to take effect.

The two-dimensional programs also have a $\boxed{\text{Blow up}}$ option under the $\boxed{\text{Task}}$ menu. In order to use it, you must first select it from the menu, then move the pointer to the upper left-hand corner of the area which you want enlarged, hold down the mouse button, drag diagonally to the bottom right-hand corner, and release the button. After you have verified your selection (by clicking on $\boxed{\text{OK}}$) the rectangle you have selected will fill the display window and in most programs the graph(s) drawn will be redrawn as well.

Another option is $\boxed{\text{Return to Default Window Bounds}}$, under the $\boxed{\text{Clear}}$ menu.

To Change Display

Use the $\boxed{\text{Settings}}$ menu to show or hide axes and/or tickmarks. Choosing $\boxed{\text{Tickmarks}}$ automatically gives you axes as well. Other options like $\boxed{\text{Colors}}$ (ANALYZER and 2D ITERATIONS) or $\boxed{\text{Slope Marks}}$ (in DIFFEQ and DIFFEQ, PHASE PLANE) will be found here.

To Change the Color of Something

Two programs, ANALYZER and 2D ITERATIONS, allow you to graph each function/orbit in a different color. These colors will also print on an Imagewriter II with multicolor ribbon, even if your screen shows only black and white.

The default setting is $\boxed{\text{Cycle Color}}$, where you will cycle through six colors: black, magenta, blue, red, green, cyan, in that order.

You can also select the color of the *next* orbit and cycle colors starting there. If you remove the check mark on the $\boxed{\text{Cycle Color}}$ the color will be fixed.

To Print the Graph

Most programs can print either directly to an Imagewriter II or to a LaserWriter through AppleTalk or a network, but only DIFFEQ, 3D VIEWS has Postscript capability for nice smooth graphs on the LaserWriter; the others are bitmapped or drawn by QuickDraw. This accounts for the jiggles in most of the output.

These programs also have an option to $\boxed{\text{Print to File}}$ under the $\boxed{\text{File}}$ menu if you need to do your printing later. When you print to a file, you will have to pick a title for the file. At the time when you wish to print, choose $\boxed{\text{File Printer}}$ from the Macintosh™ startup menu, and select the title of your file from the list on the screen.

To Use a Graph in a Picture

Choose $\boxed{\text{Copy Graph}}$, $\boxed{\text{Copy}}$, or a variation thereof from the $\boxed{\text{Edit}}$ menu, which copies the graph (the image currently on the screen) to the clipboard. The graph can then be pasted into a scrapbook (under the menu) or used in a graphics program, such as MacPaint® or SuperPaint®, where you can then edit the result, print it, insert it in a text document, or save it onto the disk for future use.

Another option for transporting graphics is to press $\boxed{\text{Shift } \mathcal{H} \text{ 3}}$ (shift-command-three), which saves the contents of the entire screen. It is stored on the current disk as a MacPaint® file, titled "Screen" with a number from 0 to 9 after it. You can use this screen dump by loading it into MacPaint® or into another graphics program which accepts MacPaint® files. Then you can erase the parts of it that you don't want and work with the rest. If you're using a Mac II, the monitor must be set to black and white. Furthermore on a Mac II the screen will be saved sideways. To see it right side up, you can select the portions you want and $\boxed{\text{Rotate}}$ them (usually an option under the $\boxed{\text{Edit}}$ menu).

Be careful about letting too many screens pile up on a disk, otherwise after you've saved "Screen 9", you will not be able to save any more screens on that disk, unless you quit the program and give different names to the various screen files. It's usually helpful to jot down on paper appropriate names for the screens as you save them.

It is important to note that sometimes a picture can be distorted, often significantly, when it is reduced. For example, text might have to be typed in again, in a smaller font, rather than reduced, in order to retain legibility.

To Use a Graph in a Text Document

As above, copy the graph into a graphics program, either by using $\boxed{\text{Copy Graph}}$ or $\boxed{\text{Shift}\ \mathcal{H}\ 3}$. Then add borders, axis titles, graph titles, bounds, or whatever else you need to make the graphic comprehensible in your document. After saving a backup to the disk, select the whole graphic and use the $\boxed{\text{Copy}}$ option to copy the end result into the scrapbook (under the ⬤ menu). Exit the graphics program and enter the text file or the text processor that you would like the picture to appear in. Then $\boxed{\text{Paste}}$ the picture where you want it to appear.

To Store Equations to Disk (or Retrieve Them)

To save, choose $\boxed{\text{Save}}$ as under the $\boxed{\text{File}}$ menu, which saves the equation(s) under the name of your choice, with its window coordinates and stepsize for the approximate solutions. It will not save the current picture (except in DIFFEQ, 3D VIEWS).

To retrieve a saved file, you must first open the appropriate application and then choose $\boxed{\text{Open}}$ under the $\boxed{\text{File}}$ menu; a list of names of previously saved equations will appear. If you double-click on a name in the "open" list, the equation will be loaded back in.

If you try to open the saved file directly by double clicking on it, it may open the application but will not load in the file. You can take care of that, direct from the application, by using $\boxed{\text{Open}}$ in the $\boxed{\text{File}}$ menu and opening your file there.

To Clear a Window

All the programs except EIGENFINDER and JACOBIDRAW have a $\boxed{\text{Clear}}$ menu, under which are several options for clearing windows. Many programs also list an option to $\boxed{\text{Erase the Last Drawn Solution, Trajectory, or Iteration}}$.

To Exit any Program

Choose $\boxed{\text{Quit}}$ under the $\boxed{\text{File}}$ menu, which returns you to the Macintosh™ startup screen. In addition, many programs have a $\boxed{\text{Quit Program}}$ option in the first screen that comes up.

Other Hints for Using MacMath Programs

- Any doubly outlined button in a dialog box can be activated by the $\boxed{\text{Return}}$ key instead of the mouse, such as most $\boxed{\text{OK}}$ boxes.

- For dialog boxes with several entries, you can use the $\boxed{\text{Tab}}$ (not $\boxed{\text{Return}}$) key to move from one entry to the next. If you hit $\boxed{\text{Return}}$ too soon, you will get an error message. Use $\boxed{\text{Return}}$ only when you are completely done.

- If you see **NAN** followed by a numeric code anywhere you expected to see a number, it means that whatever you were calculating is going to plus or minus infinity, for example, if you were dividing by zero somewhere. **NAN** stands for "not a number".

- Most items under the $\boxed{\text{Edit}}$ menu are disabled unless you are using a $\boxed{\text{Desk Accessory}}$ from the $\bullet$ menu.

- Many menu options have ⌘ and a letter next to them. The following is a list of common keyboard shortcuts, but individual programs may have additional ones:

ADD something	$\boxed{\text{⌘ A}}$
BLOW UP	$\boxed{\text{⌘ B}}$
COPY	$\boxed{\text{⌘ C}}$
DRAW something	$\boxed{\text{⌘ D}}$
CHANGE EQUATION	$\boxed{\text{⌘ E}}$
FIND something	$\boxed{\text{⌘ F}}$
COPY GRAPH	$\boxed{\text{⌘ G}}$
ITERATE	$\boxed{\text{⌘ I}}$

LOCATE SINGULARITY $\mathcal{H}$ L

CHANGE MATRIX $\mathcal{H}$ M

OPEN $\mathcal{H}$ O

PRINT something $\mathcal{H}$ P

QUIT PROGRAM $\mathcal{H}$ Q

REMOVE something $\mathcal{H}$ R

SAVE AS $\mathcal{H}$ S

RESET whatever $\mathcal{H}$ T

CLEAR/ERASE ALL $\mathcal{H}$ U

PASTE $\mathcal{H}$ V

CUT $\mathcal{H}$ X

ERASE LAST whatever $\mathcal{H}$ Y

UNDO $\mathcal{H}$ Z

EXIT whatever $\mathcal{H}$.

All the programs have the following menu bar:

FILE	EDIT	CHANGE	TASKS	SETTINGS	CLEAR

On the following page is a list of common menu elements, but individual programs will have additional ones.

FILE		EDIT		CHANGE		TASKS	
Open	⌘ O	Undo	⌘ Z	Equation	⌘ E	Draw...	⌘ D
Save As	⌘ S	— — — —	—	Matrix	⌘ M	Locate	⌘ L
— — — —	—	Cut	⌘ X	Method		Singularity	
Print to file		Copy Graph	⌘ G	Add...	⌘ A	Find...	⌘ F
Print	⌘ P	Copy	⌘ C	Remove...	⌘ R	Reset...	⌘ T
— — — —	—	Paste	⌘ V			Iterate...	⌘ I
Quit	⌘ Q					Stop Iterating	⌘ .
						Blow Up	⌘ B

SETTINGS		CLEAR	
Pause After Each Step		Graph Window	⌘ U
— — — — — — — —		Point Window	
Show Axes		Erase Last	⌘ Y
Show Tickmarks		Return to Default Bounds	

6

Analyzer

This program draws graphs of the functions of the form

$$y = f(x).$$

It also calculates the derivative of the given function, graphs it, integrates the function, finds roots, maxima and minima of the original function, and iterates the function.

Sample graph from the program ANALYZER *of the equation*

$$y = x^3 - 2x^2 + 1 .$$

How It Works

You are first prompted for the function by $y =$; after the function is correctly entered, the x and y axes are displayed. In case the equation is entered incorrectly, you will be prompted again. See Section 5, **General Overview**, for more information about entering functions, and for features common to all programs.

Now choose $\boxed{\text{Draw Graph of Function}}$ from the $\boxed{\text{Tasks}}$ menu to graph the function.

Note that the graph drawn is not always perfect: the following is an actual picture from the ANALYZER program, although the x and y labels have been added later.

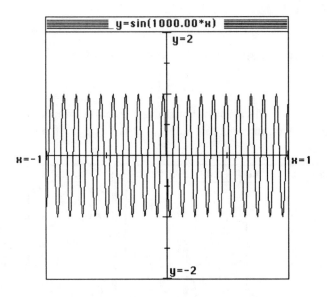

Incorrect graph from the ANALYZER *program of the function*
$$y = \sin 1000x.$$

As you can see, there aren't enough bends in this picture to make it the graph of $\sin 1000x$. The reason is that there are only 300 pixels across the screen, so the computer plots only 300 points – not enough to give a true picture of this graph.

The Equations

ANALYZER can handle up to six different functions at any one time. They are listed on the [Change] menu, in the colors in which they will be graphed.

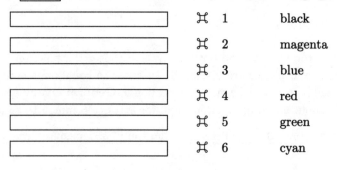

The function that is currently active has its equation at the top of the drawing window. You can activate a function either by choosing it from the $\boxed{\text{Change}}$ menu or pressing its ⌘-number key combination. Tasks are always performed on the active function.

Also on the $\boxed{\text{Change}}$ menu are the options to add or remove a function, or to edit or change the active function.

To Add a Function

To add a function select $\boxed{\text{Add Function}}$ from the $\boxed{\text{Change}}$ menu or press $\boxed{\text{⌘ A}}$. Your new function will be put in the first available slot. If you already have six functions listed, there is no available slot and $\boxed{\text{Add Function}}$ is inactive. You must then $\boxed{\text{Remove}}$ or $\boxed{\text{Edit}}$ an existing function.

To Get Another Equation in the Graph Window Bar

Choose from the $\boxed{\text{Change}}$ menu.

To Change the Equation in the Graph Window Bar

Use $\boxed{\text{⌘ E}}$ to call up the $y =$ window.

Other Features

To Graph the Function

Choose the equation from the $\boxed{\text{Change}}$ menu, or by its command equivalent. Then choose $\boxed{\text{Draw Graph of Function}}$ from the $\boxed{\text{Tasks}}$ menu.

To Draw the Derivative

Choose the equation from the $\boxed{\text{Change}}$ menu. Choose $\boxed{\text{Draw Derivative}}$ from the $\boxed{\text{Tasks}}$ menu. The program will symbolically calculate the derivative, display it in the title of the drawing window, and draw the graph of $y = df/dx$.

$\boxed{\text{Draw Graph}}$ and $\boxed{\text{Draw Derivative}}$ will superimpose the new graph on top of the graphs that are already on the screen, which allows comparison of the graphs of different functions. To erase a graph use $\boxed{\text{Hide Graph}}$ from the $\boxed{\text{Tasks}}$ menu or select an appropriate option from the $\boxed{\text{Clear}}$ menu.

To Integrate

The desired function should be displayed in the Graph Window Bar. Select $\boxed{\text{Integrate}}$ from the $\boxed{\text{Tasks}}$ menu. Then choose a method. The area under the graph from left bound to right bound is numerically calculated and displayed in a window to the right of the screen. If you don't want to have the integration panels drawn, uncheck Draw Integration Method on the Settings menu.

The Number of Panels for Integration can be changed under the Change menu.

To Find the Roots of the Graph

First, select the function as explained above. Then choose Find Roots from the Task menu. The roots of the original entered function (if they exist) will be displayed in the Root(s) window. You will be given a choice between two methods:

- **Bisection method** will find all at once the roots on the screen by looking for places where the function goes from positive to negative and narrowing in on the root. How close it comes to the root is determined by the Tolerance for Bisection, which you can change using the Change menu. However, this method can miss a root where the graph does not actually cross the x-axis, as at the point $(0,0)$ in the first example pictured.

- **Newton's method** will find the roots that the Bisection method misses plus others not necessarily in the window, but for each individual root you have to make an initial guess, by positioning the cursor on the x-axis and clicking the mouse. The method works by taking the tangent line to the function $f(x_0)$ for the given x-coordinate, x_0, and following this tangent down to where it crosses the x-axis at x_1, then repeating the process with the new x-value and $f(x_1)$ to get x_2. The process continues until the x_i's converge on a limit (to the desired tolerance). Newton's method converges very fast, approximately doubling the number of correct digits at each step.

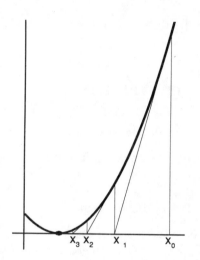

Diagram of how
Newton's Method works.

After you have chosen a method, the roots of the selected function (if they exist) will be displayed in the Root(s) window.

To Mark the Roots and the Maxima and Minima

Select the function from the Change menu and Find Roots from the Tasks menu. You may choose between Bisection and Newton's methods. This option will highlight roots with a black circle.

To Find the Maxima and Minima

Select the function from the Change menu and Find Maxima-Minima from the Tasks menu. Maxima and/or minima of the original entered function (if they exist) will be displayed in the Min/Max window, which appears in place of the Root(s) window. You may choose the method from the same two options as finding roots. The extrema will be highlighted with a gray circle.

To Iterate an Equation

Select the function from the Change menu and Iterate ... from the Tasks menu. This program will draw the graph of the function in the Graph Window Bar and the graph of the diagonal $y = x$. After that, you may click the mouse anywhere in the drawing window to begin iterating at that x-position.

The program will perform the iterations Step by Step (requiring you to tap the space bar for every iteration) or Continuously, which you choose in the dialog box for Iterate ... To stop iterating, click the mouse once.

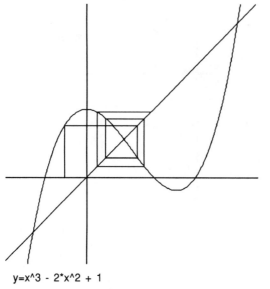

x=-0.32332
y=0.75713
- - - - - - - - - - -
x=0.75713
y=0.28753
- - - - - - - - - - -
x=0.28753
y=0.85843
- - - - - - - - - - -
x=0.85843
y=0.15878
- - - - - - - - - - -
x=0.15878
y=0.95358
- - - - - - - - - - -

y=x^3 - 2*x^2 + 1
-1.22074 < x < 2.55853
-1.25418 < y < 2.52508

Sample graph from the ANALYZER *program of an iteration of the equation* $y = x^3 - 2x^2 + 1$.

To See a Numerical List of Iterates

This option is available either for finding roots by Newton's method, or for iteration. Clear the Min/Max or Roots window, then check, under the Settings menu, either Show Newton's Approximations or See Iteration Values. The List window will now be headed by Approx. Roots or Iteration, respectively.

To Clear the List Window

Choose Clear List Window from the Clear menu, whichever list is currently on the screen: Roots, Min/Max, Approx. Root(s), or Iterations.

To Change the Displayed Number of Digits

Choose Number of Decimal Digits Displayed from the Change menu, which tells how many digits are to be displayed in the Root(s) or Min/Max window; the default is 5 (if you choose 7 or 8, one or more digits may be hidden at the right side of the window).

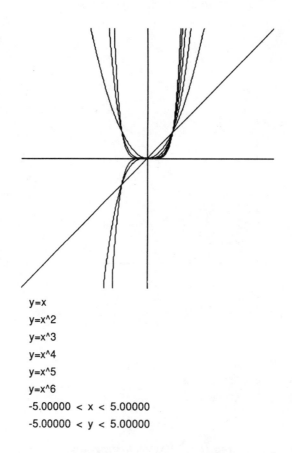

y=x
y=x^2
y=x^3
y=x^4
y=x^5
y=x^6
-5.00000 < x < 5.00000
-5.00000 < y < 5.00000

Sample ANALYZER *printout.*

Some Examples to Explore

Try ANALYZER **on the following:**

1. Compare $y = x$, $y = x^2$, $y = x^3$, $y = x^4$, $y = x^5$, $y = x^6$. What can you predict about $y = x^n$?

2. Compare $y = \sin(1/x)$, $y = x\sin(1/x)$, $y = x^2\sin(1/x)$. Make blowups to examine what happens around $x = 0$.

3. Graph $y = \sin 2x + \cos x/2$. Try other combinations of the form $y = \sin nx + \cos mx$. What sort of prediction can you make?

4. Graph $y = 2\sin x + 3\cos x$. Try other combinations of the form $y = k\sin x + j\cos x$. What sort of prediction can you make? Try combining the ideas of Experiments #3 and #4.

5. Try $y = \sqrt[3]{x} = x^{1/3}$ by entering y = x ^ (1/3).
Note: You won't get as much of the graph as you might expect, because the ^ command tells the computer to use logarithms in calculating powers – this won't work for negative x.

6. Graph $y = \dfrac{\sin 20x}{\sin x}$, an approximation to the Dirichlet kernel. (The n-th Dirichlet kernel is actually $D_n(x) = \dfrac{1}{2\pi}\dfrac{\sin((2n+1)x/2)}{\sin(x/2)}$.)

7. Graph
$$y = x \ ;$$
$$\text{then} \quad y = x - \frac{x^3}{6} \ ;$$
$$\text{then} \quad y = x - \frac{x^3}{6} + \frac{x^5}{120} \ ;$$
$$\text{then} \quad y = x - \frac{x^3}{6} + \frac{x^5}{120} - \frac{x^7}{720} \ ,$$

and so on, alternating signs as you add terms of the form $x^n/n!$ for odd n. Do you recognize the function for which this sequence approximates the Taylor series?

8. Graph
$$y = \sin x \ ;$$
$$\text{then} \quad y = \sin x - \frac{\sin 3x}{3} \ ;$$
$$\text{then} \quad y = \sin x - \frac{\sin 3x}{3} + \frac{\sin 5x}{5} \ ; \quad \dots$$

Do you recognize the function for which this sequence approximates the Fourier series?

9.   Repeat the previous example using $\dfrac{\sin nx}{n^2}$ instead of $\dfrac{\sin nx}{n}$.

10.   Enter the function $f(x) = 5 - x^2/5$, and use the command $\boxed{\text{Integrate}}$ to compute the integral (the exact value is 33.333 ...). Now vary the number of grid points, to verify that the approximation improves as the number of grid points increases. Now vary the method of integration to see how much faster Simpson's method converges than the other methods. (You may be surprised by how remarkably fast Simpson's method does converge. For quadratic and cubic polynomials, Simpson's method is in fact exact.)

11.   Now try to compute

$$\int_0^{\pi/2} \cos x \, dx \ .$$

Enter the function $\cos x$ as usual, and set low x to be 0, and high x to be $\pi/2$. Again try varying the numbers of grid points, and the method of integration.

12.   Use the roots algorithm to compute $\sqrt{2}$. You can do this by entering the function $x^2 - 2$, and using the $\boxed{\text{Find Roots}}$ command. Now try to find the solutions of $x^3 + x + 1 = 0$, and the solutions of $\sin x = x/2$.

13.   For each of the following functions,

$$x^2 - 1.76 \ , \qquad x^2 - 2 \ , \qquad 2x^2 - 1 \ ,$$

examine the behavior under iteration, and note the differences.

14.   Consider the function $f(x) = x^3 - 2x + \alpha$. In each of the cases $\alpha = 2$ and $\alpha = 1.9$, try finding the roots by Newton's method, starting at $x_0 = $ zero (get as close to $x = $ zero as you can by watching the point window as you move the mouse, holding its button down). Note the differences in behavior, and in the table of roots iterates. If you set $\boxed{\text{Draw Newton's Tangent}}$ under the $\boxed{\text{Settings}}$ menu, you may see better why you sometimes get a cycle. Try other values of α between 2 and 1.9, like 1.95.

7

DiffEq

This program prints a slope field and draws solutions in the tx-plane for a differential equation of the form

$$\frac{dx}{dt} = f(t, x) \ .$$

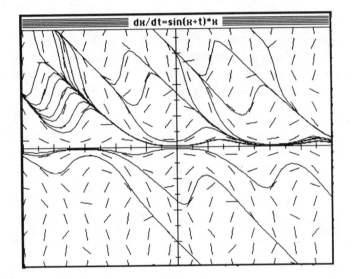

Sample graph from the DiffEq program. The dashes make up the slope field, the curves are sample solutions to the differential equation

$$\frac{dx}{dt} = x\sin(x + t) \ .$$

How It Works

At the prompt $dx/dt =$, enter a function in x and t. Press Return to go on. See Section 5, **General Overview**, for more information about entering functions, and for features common to all programs.

Now you'll see a blank screen, and you'll probably want to see the slope field of your differential equation. You can bring it up by choosing Slope Marks under Settings . You can also bring up axes and tickmarks by appropriate choices under Settings . Choosing Tickmarks will automatically give you axes as well.

You may then select, using the mouse, an initial point in the tx-plane through which a solution is to be drawn. The small window at the top right corner of the screen displays the coordinates of the arrow tip if the mouse button is held down with the cursor in the drawing window. When you release the button, the drawing of the solution begins in the forward ($+t$) direction. When the solution reaches the edge of the window, the program returns to the initial point and draws the solution in the backwards ($-t$) direction.

Initial points may be selected as often as desired. Drawing that is in progress can be terminated at any time by clicking on the screen, once to stop forward drawing, again to stop backward drawing.

If you'd like to try a different equation, choose Change Equation from the Change menu.

To print a graph, make sure your printer is properly connected and turned on. Then choose Print Graph from the File menu to get a preformatted copy of the graph, equation, and bounds. See Section 5, **General Overview**, for more information on printing, saving the graph, and related topics.

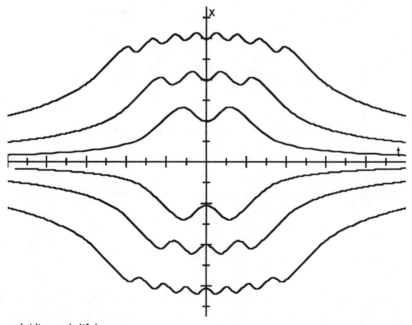

dx/dt = sin(t*x)
-7.500 < x < 7.500
-10.000 < t < 10.000

Sample DIFFEQ *printout.*

Other Features

To Pause After Each Step and Display the Coordinates of the Point:

Choose $\boxed{\text{Display Point After Each Step}}$ from the $\boxed{\text{Settings}}$ menu, then press the spacebar to go through the points. Hold the spacebar down for continuous steps. The coordinates of the approximate solution, after each step, will be displayed in the $\boxed{\text{Points}}$ window.

To Change the Approximation Method

The default method that the program uses to calculate trajectories is Runge-Kutta. Choose $\boxed{\text{Change Method}}$ under the $\boxed{\text{Change}}$ menu and click on Euler or Midpoint Euler to change it.

To Remove Slope Marks from the Screen

Click on the checked $\boxed{\text{Slope Marks}}$ option under the $\boxed{\text{Settings}}$ menu to uncheck it. The computer will redraw the screen without slope marks.

To See Denser Slope Marks

Choose $\boxed{\text{Graph Window with Dense Slope Marks}}$ from the $\boxed{\text{Settings}}$ menu. This will draw about 1200 slope marks on the screen, as opposed to 225 for normal slope marks.

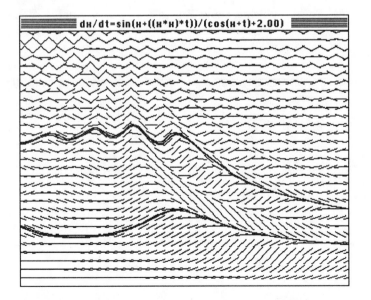

Sample graph from the DIFFEQ *program, with dense slope marks.*

If the Trajectories Make Sharp Angles or Don't Fit the Slope Field

Choose Change Step Size from the Change menu and try typing in a smaller step size, then try another trajectory. If this doesn't do the trick, consider the next hint.

To Convert Equations to Two-Dimensional Systems

The fact that very steep slopes can cause solutions to shoot off the screen is due to $x' = f(t, x)$ involving a denominator going to zero and the fact that solutions $x = u(t)$ must be single-valued functions. You can try your equation on the program DIFFEQ, PHASE PLANE instead, where the solutions x and y are found as parametric equations in t; in this case there are no problems going through vertical slope marks in the vector field.

The procedure to change a DIFFEQ equation to a system for DIFFEQ, PHASE PLANE is:

- write $x' = f(t, x)$ as $\dfrac{\text{numerator}}{\text{denominator}}$,
- change x to y, and then t to x,
- then use DIFFEQ, PHASE PLANE with $dx/dt =$ denominator, $dy/dt =$ numerator.

Example 7.1.

$$\frac{dx}{dt} = \frac{1}{x} - t = \frac{1 - tx}{x} \qquad \text{is changed to} \qquad \frac{dy}{dx} = \frac{1 - xy}{y}$$

$$\text{which is equivalent to} \qquad \frac{dx}{dt} = y \quad \text{and} \quad \frac{dy}{dt} = 1 - xy.$$

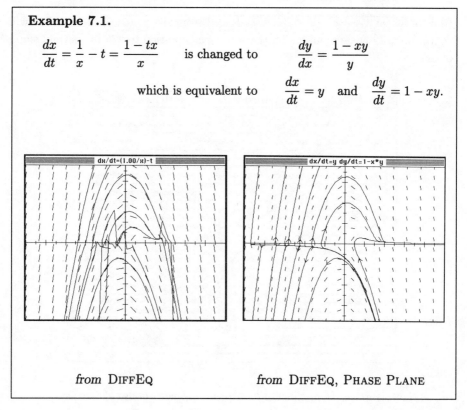

from DIFFEQ   *from* DIFFEQ, PHASE PLANE

Some Examples to Explore

Try DiffEq on the following:

1. Try the following differential equations and note how "small" changes in the functions make dramatic changes in the slope fields and behavior of solutions.

$$\frac{dx}{dt} = \frac{x}{t}, \quad \frac{dx}{dt} = \frac{t}{x}, \quad \frac{dx}{dt} = \frac{x}{2t}, \quad \frac{dx}{dt} = \frac{2x}{t}.$$

2. Enter $dx/dt = \sin(t^3 - x^3)$ and try drawing solutions. The solutions should not cross, so experiment with making the stepsize small enough that they do not.

3. A nice illustration of how successful the different methods are at drawing the solutions is to try them on $dx/dt = x$, with a stepsize of 1.0. Analytically we know the solution is $x = e^x$, so you can easily test the results with the help of a calculator. The success of Runge-Kutta even for such a ridiculous stepsize is amazing! You might want to change your window bounds; even just two steps is dramatic, so try $0 < t < 2$, and then $0 < x < 8$ will be sufficient to get above $x(2) = e^2 = 7.38905609\ldots$.

4. Enter $dx/dt = x^2 - t$, which cannot be solved by traditional analytic methods, and draw some trajectories. See what predictions you can make about the solutions, depending on the initial condition. Try changing the t bounds to run higher (e.g., for a stepsize of 0.3, try high $t = 15$). In such a case you will find your solution drawings breaking down before they get all the way to the right. Try the different methods of drawing the solutions – you'll find that all of them go awry eventually, although sometimes it's not obvious at first that some "solutions" are spurious.

5. Enter $dx/dt = \sin(tx)$, which cannot be solved by traditional analytic methods, and draw some trajectories. If they get too jagged, try a smaller stepsize. See what predictions you can make about the solutions, depending on the initial condition.

6. Repeat the previous exercise using $dx/dt = t\sin(tx); \quad dx/dt = x\sin(tx)$.

You might use ANALYZER to print out a picture of some *isoclines*, curves that show where the slopes defined by the differential equation do not change. For example, in Experiment 4 above, you can make the following comparison with a DiffEq printout.

The solutions to the differential equation will have *zero* slope where $x^2 - t = 0$ which you can enter in ANALYZER as y = $\sqrt{x}$ and y = $-\sqrt{x}$.

The isoclines for slope *one* are $x^2 - t = 1$, so you would enter into ANALYZER the equations y = $\sqrt{x+1}$ and y = - $\sqrt{x+1}$.

The isoclines for slope *negative one* are $x^2 - t = -1$, so you would enter into ANALYZER the equations y = $\sqrt{x-1}$ and y = - $\sqrt{x-1}$.

Set the window bounds on ANALYZER to match the vertical bounds on your DIFFEQ printout. For example, if your DIFFEQ vertical axis runs from -7.5 to 7.5, set the ANALYZER (square) window bounds to run from -7.5 to 7.5 in both directions.

Select $\boxed{\text{Show Graph}}$ for all the functions you've selected in ANALYZER, and $\boxed{\text{Print}}$ the graph.

You can draw on your ANALYZER printout appropriate little slope marks for the differential equation and then hold this printout up to the light with a DIFFEQ printout with a number of trajectories to see that the solutions should indeed match with the isocline information.

8

Numerical Methods

This program calculates the numerical solution of the differential equation of the form

$$\frac{dx}{dt} = f(t, x)$$

using any of the three numerical methods: Euler, Midpoint Euler, or Runge-Kutta. In order to analyze the error in a given method, the program also calculates the error and "order", and can graph the error as a function of the step size.

Steps	Euler	Order=p
2^0	2.000000000000e+0	
2^1	2.250000000000e+0	
2^2	2.441406250000e+0	-0.8202
2^3	2.565784513950e+0	1.8274
2^4	2.637928497046e+0	0.7858
2^5	2.676990129985e+0	0.8851
2^6	2.697344956920e+0	0.9404
2^7	2.707739015110e+0	0.9696
2^8	2.712991628796e+0	0.9847
2^9	2.715632005595e+0	0.9923
2^10	2.716955719516e+0	0.9962

(window title: dx/dt=x)

Sample approximate solutions from the NUMERICAL METHODS *program for the differential equation* $\frac{dx}{dt} = x$.

How It Works

At the prompt $\frac{dx}{dt} =$, enter a function in x and t. After the equation has been entered, press ⟨Return⟩. See Section 5, **General Overview**, for more information about entering functions, and for features common to all programs.

Choose the option ⟨Solve Numerically⟩ under the ⟨Tasks⟩ menu, and the program will attempt to find the value of the solution at a given point t (⟨Final t⟩) for a

53

specified initial condition ($\boxed{\text{Init } t}$ and $\boxed{\text{Init } x}$ in the Initial Condition window) given a specified limit on the length of each number it works with ($\boxed{\# \text{ Bits}}$) and a rounding method ($\boxed{\text{Trunc}}$). It will do this by breaking up the interval between $\boxed{\text{Init } t}$ and $\boxed{\text{Final } t}$ into a number (always a power of 2) of subintervals ($\boxed{\text{Steps}}$), and for each power of 2 calculating an approximate solution.

Warning: This program is very susceptible to crashing on a Macintosh™ smaller than a Mac II, because the calculations are not checked for division by zero or for being out of range.

Other Features

To Change Initial Conditions

Click in boxes $\boxed{\text{Init } t}$ and $\boxed{\text{Init } x}$ in the Initial Condition window and type in new values to specify the initial point. $\boxed{\text{Final } t}$ specifies the t-coordinate of the final point. $\boxed{\text{Sol'n}}$ should be left $\boxed{?}$ if you do not know the exact numerical solution. The program then will calculate a bound on the error from the value at k steps compared with the value at $2k$ steps. However, if the exact solution is known, and entered numerically, exact error will be calculated and displayed (with two digits, in scientific notation).

To Change the Approximation Method

The default method that the program uses to calculate trajectories is Runge-Kutta. Choose $\boxed{\text{Change Method}}$ under the $\boxed{\text{Change}}$ menu and click on Euler or Midpoint Euler to change it.

To Change the Number of Significant Bits

The numbers in a computer are stored in binary form, with each digit being a bit (a binary digit — 0 or 1). Since 2^{10} is 1024, ten bits are roughly equivalent to three significant digits. Click in the $\boxed{\# \text{ Bits}}$ box to change the number of bits the computer will work with. You should enter a number between 1 and 64. (For example, 32 bits, for a step-size range of 2^0 to 2^{10}, will take 2 to 3 minutes for the Runge-Kutta method.)

The remaining bits will be truncated or rounded, depending on the state of the next text box, which is $\boxed{\text{Trunc}}$. There are three choices: you can enter $\boxed{\text{Up}}$, $\boxed{\text{Down}}$, or $\boxed{\text{Round}}$. Here, $\boxed{\text{Up}}$ means always round up, $\boxed{\text{Down}}$ means always round down, and $\boxed{\text{Round}}$ means round to the nearest bit.

For example, 0.111101_{Binary} (0.953125_{Ten}), to four digits, would round *up* to 1.0000_{Binary} (1.0000_{Ten}), *down* to 0.1111_{Binary} (0.9375_{Ten}), and *round* to 0.1111_{Binary} (again, 0.9375_{Ten}).

After you have finished with the Initial Condition dialog box, click $\boxed{\text{OK}}$.

Error Analysis

It is possible to graph the error as a function of stepsize. First solve the differential equation numerically, with some range of steps, using one of the methods in the menu. Then pull down the [Tasks] menu and choose [Graph Stepsize vs. Error]. A dialog box asking you for a stable region will come up. Enter the region where the approximate order seems to come close to some constant. After you have clicked [OK], the [Interpolation] window will show calculated values of c_0 and c_1 (Hubbard and West, *Differential Equations: A Dynamical Systems Approach*, Volume I, Chapter 3.4–3.5) using the formula

$$\text{Approximate solution} = c_0 + c_1 h^p \; ,$$

where h is the stepsize, c_0 the exact value of the solution, and p the exact order. The exact *order* refers to the method used – Euler's method, the default, is first order, Midpoint Euler second order, and Runge-Kutta is a fourth order method. As the approximate solution gets more and more accurate, the approximate order should get closer and closer to one, two, or four, respectively.

Then you will see two graphs in the [Graph] window. The first one is plotting the points (h, approximate solution) which you have just calculated. The other one (gray) is using the above interpolation to graph the linear approximation to the approximate solution, as a function of h.

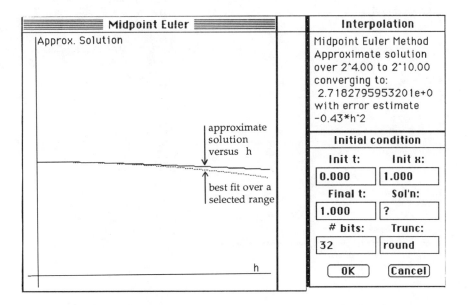

Sample graph of approximate solution versus h from the NUMERICAL METHODS *program, using Euler's method, and the equation*

$$\frac{dx}{dt} = x \sin(x) \cos(x + t).$$

dx/dt = x

Steps	Euler	Order=p
2^0	2.000000000000e+0	
2^1	2.250000000000e+0	
2^2	2.441406250000e+0	-0.8202
2^3	2.565784513950e+0	1.8274
2^4	2.637928497046e+0	0.7858
2^5	2.676990129985e+0	0.8851
2^6	2.697344956920e+0	0.9404
2^7	2.707739015110e+0	0.9696
2^8	2.712991628796e+0	0.9847
2^9	2.715632005595e+0	0.9923
2^10	2.716955719516e+0	0.9962

Initial t: 0.000
Final t: 1.000
Initial x: 1.000
Number of bits: 32
Truncation Method: round
No solution given

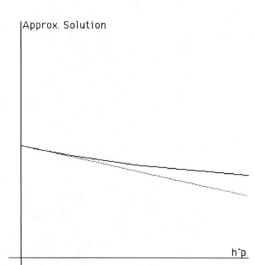

Approx. Solution

h^p

Euler's Method
Approximate solution
over 2^3.00 to 2^10.00
converging to:
   2.7170160741262e+0
with error estimate
-1.22*h

Sample NUMERICAL METHODS *printout.*

Some Examples to Explore

Try NUMERICAL METHODS **on the following:**

1.   A nice illustration of how successful the different methods are at drawing the solutions is to try them on $dx/dt = x$, for $x_0 = 1$ when $t_0 = 0$ and $t_f = 2$. Analytically we know the solution is $x = e^x$, so you can easily test the results by the fact that $x(2) = e^2 \approx 7.38905609\ldots$ The success of Runge-Kutta even for large stepsize is amazing!

2.   Try $dx/dt = x^2$, for $x_0 = 1$ when $t_0 = -1$, and $t_f = 1$. You may not think anything is strange yet. Try it both for Euler's method and Runge-Kutta, and compare. Now do you think something might be wrong? Note that the solution is $x = -1/t$ (if you don't believe this, try differentiating this solution and observe that it indeed satisfies the differential equation, as does any function of the form $x = 1/(c - t)$), so there is a vertical asymptote at $t = 0$. Does the numerical approximation take that into account? Why? Is the problem solvable by a smaller stepsize? Why? Can you think of ways to avoid this trap? (**MacMath** doesn't, alas!)

3.   Try $dx/dt = x^2 \sin t$, for $x_0 = 0.3$ when $t_0 = 0$, and $t_f = \pi$, for each of the three approximation methods. Note that the orders settle down around the expected values of 1, 2, and 4 for Euler, midpoint Euler, and Runge-Kutta, respectively. Note also that if you go far enough, the "order" eventually destabilizes; this will happen most quickly for the Runge-Kutta method.

4.   Now repeat the previous experiment changing t_f to 2π. This time you will find different "orders" for midpoint Euler and Runge-Kutta, because the solution $x = 1/(\cos t + c)$ is periodic over the interval 0 to 2π . (We know that $x(2\pi) = x(0) = 0.3$.) This surprise happens because the solution is *symmetric* over the interval, which was not the case in the previous experiment.

5.   Experiment with the effects of different kinds of rounding (e.g., down versus round), and cut the number of bits (e.g., to 18) to more readily observe the effects. A simple example to try is $x' = x$, from $x_0 = 1$ when $t_0 = 0$ to $t_f = 2$. You should notice that the expected order appears quite briefly and, in the case of rounding up or down, later settles down about an order of -1, due to the fact that in these cases error $\approx c_1 h P + c_2/h$.

9
DiffEq, Phase Plane

This program prints a direction field and draws trajectories in the x, y-phase plane for an autonomous system of differential equations of the form

$$\frac{dx}{dt} = f(x, y) \quad \text{and} \quad \frac{dy}{dt} = g(x, y)$$

and locates and analyzes singularities.

Note: Autonomous means that dx/dt and dy/dt are only functions of x and y, not of t.

Furthermore, two parameters, a and b, may be included in the equations in order to explore where bifurcations occur. So far the program can locate in ab-parameter space the locus for sink-source bifurcation and for saddle-node bifurcation.

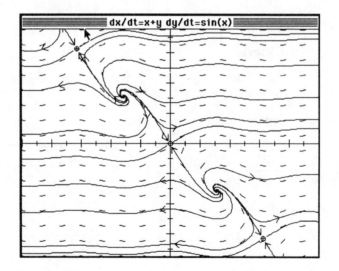

Sample graph from the DIFFEQ, PHASE PLANE program. The dashes make up the slope field, the curves are sample trajectories to the system of differential equations

$$\frac{dx}{dt} = x + y , \qquad \frac{dy}{dt} = \sin(x).$$

Note that the initial points are marked by arrows showing the direction of the trajectory as t increases.

How It Works

When first prompted for the equations in DIFFEQ, PHASE PLANE, enter functions that depend only on x and y, but not on t, because only in the autonomous case does the phase plane make good sense. Please refer to Section 5, **General Overview**, for instructions on entering functions and on features common to all programs.

To Draw a Solution

Choose Draw trajectory from the Tasks menu, then select a point through which a trajectory is to be drawn by moving the cursor to the point of interest and clicking. Drawing proceeds first in the positive time direction and then in the negative direction (which by default is computed by a fourth order Runge-Kutta method). At any time while drawing is in progress, you can terminate the process by clicking the mouse. The first click stops the forward direction, the second click stops the backward direction. Therefore you will have to click twice if you want to interrupt while drawing is proceeding in the forward time direction. You have the option to Change Step Size under the Change menu.

Other Features

To Observe Slope Marks

Use the Settings menu to choose or remove slope marks, or to choose Denser Slope Marks, as in the DIFFEQ program.

To Change the Approximation Method

The default method that the program uses to calculate trajectories is Runge-Kutta. Choose Change Method under the Change menu and click on Euler or Midpoint Euler to change it.

To Locate a Singularity

Choose Locate Singularity. Under this option, you click near a point where you think a singularity exists (a point where dx/dt and dy/dt are zero). The program locates a singularity (if there is one) using Newton's method (with the clicked location as the starting point) and displays a message indicating the type of the singularity. The singularity is also noted on the graph by an appropriate symbol:

○ *spiral source*	□ *spiral sink*	⊙ *center*
● *node source*	■ *node sink*	⊕ *saddle point*

If the singularity is a saddle point, then the separatrices are drawn from that point. If no singularity is found after 100 Newton iterations, or if the mouse is clicked while the search is in progress, a message will appear saying that no singularity has been found. To find another singularity, first click anywhere in the drawing window to get rid of the message, and then click at the point where you want a new search to start.

Note: Newton's method does not always converge to the closest singularity. Furthermore, sometimes the program does not locate a singularity when it should, or it fails to report its type accurately. This may occur if the singularities are too close together, if the singularity is a border case between two different types, or if the equations have been changed too many times (in which case a restart may work). Finally, we note that the bifurcation algorithms may crash the program if the equations are too long.

Special Section on Bifurcation

The DIFFEQ, PHASE PLANE program can be used to study bifurcation with two parameters, a and b, as discussed in Sections 18 and 19 of this documentation, and more thoroughly in Chapter 9 of Hubbard and West, *Differential Equations: A Dynamical Systems Approach*, Volume II. The idea is that there exists a curve in ab-space where a given type of bifurcation occurs (that is, a drastic change in xy-space of the behavior of solutions), and the program locates and draws such a curve in the ab-parameter space.

The following types of bifurcations (Section 19) are classified by the linearization (Section 18) of the vector field at a singularity, and are now incorporated in the program.

The Sink-Source Bifurcation Locus

This consists of the points in parameter space where at a singularity of the differential equation the trace of the linearization is zero and the determinant of the linearization is positive, thus representing the division between sinks and sources (see Section 18 on predicting behavior for linear differential equations).

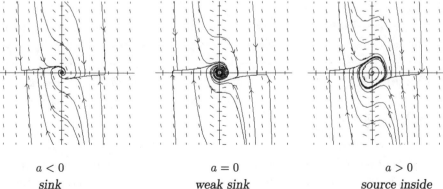

| $a < 0$ | $a = 0$ | $a > 0$ |
| sink | weak sink | source inside limit cycle |

The typical result is that as a point (a, b) in the parameter plane moves toward the bifurcation locus, a sink (or source) in the xy-plane becomes, at bifurcation, a weak sink (or source) and then, after bifurcation, becomes a limit cycle with the opposite equilibrium point, i.e., a source (or sink), at the center. This phenomenon is called *Hopf bifurcation*.

But it may also be the case that a source is just exchanged with a sink without creating a limit cycle, as in Example 9.1 below.

The Saddle-Node Bifurcation Locus

This consists of the points in parameter space where the differential equation has a singularity and the determinant of the linearization is zero, thus representing the division between saddles and nodes (see Section 18 on linearization and predicting behavior for linear differential equations).

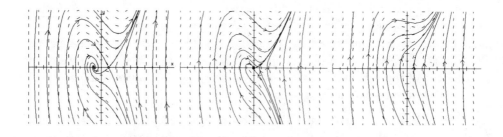

$a < 0$	$a = 0$	$a > 0$
source and saddle	*node and saddle*	*no more*
	coalesce	*singularities*

Crossing the bifurcation locus in parameter space means that in xy-space a saddle and a node typically coalesce. Before bifurcation a node and a saddle both exist separately; at bifurcation the two zeroes coincide; after bifurcation there are no longer any zeroes of the vector field, so the node and saddle simply disappear.

But it may also be the case that a saddle is simply exchanged with a node without any coalescing taking place.

Example 9.1.   The linear differential equation $dx/dt = x - ay$, $dy/dt = ax + by$ has the unique singularity $(x, y) = (0, 0)$ with the linearization matrix:

$$\begin{pmatrix} 1 & -a \\ a & b \end{pmatrix}.$$

The determinant is $b + a^2$ and the trace is $1 + b$. So the sink-source bifurcation locus is that part of the horizontal line $b = -1$ which lies outside the parabola, $b = -a^2$, while the saddle-node bifurcation locus consists of the parameter points lying on the parabola $b = -a^2$.

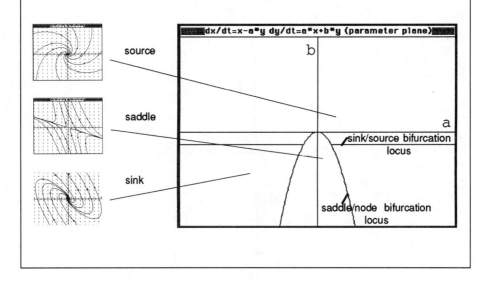

How to Use the Bifurcation Features

You may enter parameters a and b in your differential equation. The default values are $a = 1$ and $b = 1$, but you can change them with $\boxed{\text{Change Parameters}}$ in the $\boxed{\text{Change}}$ menu. You may also switch to the $\boxed{\text{Parameter Plane}}$ under the $\boxed{\text{Settings}}$ menu, and change them graphically.

To Locate A Sink-Source Bifurcation

Choose $\boxed{\text{Locate Sink-Source Bifurcation}}$. Click at the singularity that you expect to bifurcate, as in the option to $\boxed{\text{Locate Singularities}}$. The screen switches to the *parameter plane*, where the parameter point expands to a circle until the circle hits a bifurcation point. Then the program traces out the bifurcation locus in the *ab*-parameter space.

To Locate A Saddle-Node Bifurcation

Choose $\boxed{\text{Saddle-Node Bifurcation}}$. Again you click at the singularity that you expect to bifurcate; the program constructs the locus of the saddle-node bifurcation in *ab*-parameter space.

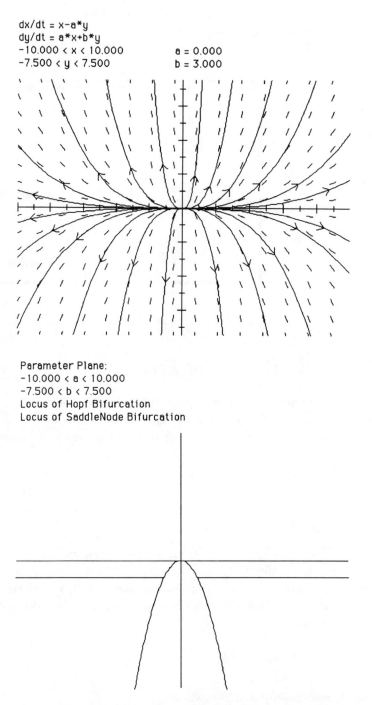

dx/dt = x−a*y
dy/dt = a*x+b*y
−10.000 < x < 10.000   a = 0.000
−7.500 < y < 7.500   b = 3.000

Parameter Plane:
−10.000 < a < 10.000
−7.500 < b < 7.500
Locus of Hopf Bifurcation
Locus of SaddleNode Bifurcation

Sample printout from DiffEq, Phase Plane.

Some Examples to Explore

Try DIFFEQ, PHASE PLANE **on the following:**

1. Try $dx/dt = \sin(x+y)$, $dy/dt = \cos(xy)$. Draw some trajectories, then use the $\boxed{\text{Locate Singularity}}$ task to pinpoint and identify sinks, sources, and saddles. You should also be able to see some *limit cycles* in your drawing, although the program does not find them.

2. Try a predator-prey system $dx/dt = (2-y)x$ and $dy/dt = (0.3x-0.7)y$. Draw some trajectories and locate the equilibrium. (Refer to Example 3 in Section 3, **Iteration.**) Then see what happens if you add a little fishing or hunting. That is, let $dx/dt = (2-y)x - ax$ and $dy/dt = (0.3x - 0.7)y - by$, where a and b give the hunting or fishing rates for each population. How does this move the equilibrium?

Try different values for a and b, to see that you consistently get the same effect. What does it mean biologically? In fact, this model was developed by an Italian mathematician Volterra, to answer the question posed by biologist Lotka, who noticed that when Mediterranean fishing was drastically reduced during World War I, the percentage of sharks (predators) caught greatly increased; when fishing resumed, the number of food fish (prey) increased!

3. A more general model of two species interaction is given by the system $dx/dt = ax - bx^2 - cxy$ and $dy/dt = dy - ey^2 + fxy$,, where the squared terms represent crowding or competition within a species. Try different values of the parameters to see different possible long range effects. For example, each of the following values for the parameters gives a different outcome, which you can interpret in terms of the populations:

$$(a, b, c, d, e, f) \quad = \quad (1, 4, 1, 2, 1, 3)$$
$$(2, 1, 1, 1, 1, 4)$$
$$(1, 0.25, 1, 2, 1, 1)$$
$$(2, 1, 1, 1, 1, 0.25) \ .$$

4. Examine the behavior of the system $dx/dt = y$ and $dy/dt = \sin x$. Experiment with the effects of the parameter a inserted as follows: $dx/dt = y$, $dy/dt = \sin x - ay$.

5. For the system $dx/dt = x^2 - y$, $dy/dt = y - ax - b$, experiment with phase plane behavior for different values of the parameters a and b. Look for the sink-source bifurcation locus. You can interpret your results in terms of the phase plane isoclines of horizontal and vertical slope, where $dy/dt = 0$ and $dx/dt = 0$, respectively.

6.   Examine the phase plane behavior for the double potential well oscillator: $x'' = -d/dx(V(x))$; in this case the potential $V(x) = -x^2/2 + x^4/100$, so $x'' = -d/dx(V(x))$ which you write as a system $dx/dt = y$, $dy/dt = x - x^3/25$.

Suggestion: Start by graphing the potential using ANALYZER (with the bounds $-10 \leq x \leq 10$, $-20 \leq y \leq 20$), and see if you can predict the behavior of the solution curves in the phase plane.

We shall experiment further with this model in Experiment #5 of Section 13, **2D Iterations**.

7.   Van der Pol's equation $x'' + (x^2 - 1)x' + x = 0$ describes a nonlinear electric circuit with an interesting phase plane picture. Enter it as a system $dx/dt = y$, $dy/dt = (1 - x^2)y - x = 0$ and plot some trajectories, which show a nice limit cycle. This behavior can be understood if you think of Van der Pol's equation as describing a damped harmonic oscillator, with "friction" $x^2 - 1$. This "friction" is only positive for $|x| > 1$, so it produces damping only if x is large. If $|x| < 1$, the oscillator is being driven; it's not so surprising to see the phase plane motion settle down to a particular oscillation.

10

DiffEq, 3D Views

This program draws three-dimensional graphs and relevant planar graphs for either of the following:

- An *autonomous* system of differential equations of the form

$$\frac{dx}{dt} = f(x, y, z), \quad \frac{dy}{dt} = g(x, y, z), \quad \text{and} \quad \frac{dz}{dt} = h(x, y, z).$$

In this case the trajectories are drawn in xyz-space and the planar views are xy, xz, yz. The program also locates and analyzes singularities in xyz-space. (Three more planar views: xt, yt, and zt are not visible on the screen, but you can ask for the printouts to show them.)

- A *nonautonomous* system of differential equations of the form

$$\frac{dx}{dt} = f(t, x, y) \quad \text{and} \quad \frac{dy}{dt} = g(t, x, y).$$

Here the trajectories are drawn in txy-space and the planar views are xy, tx, ty. In this case the program does not locate and analyze singularities since it is setting $z = t$ (hence $dz/dt = 1$ and there can be no 3D singularities). However it allows you the choice of investigating Poincaré sections provided the nonautonomous 2D differential equations are periodic in t. This will be explained at the end of this section.

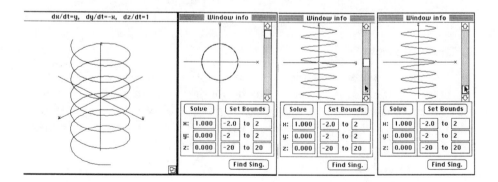

Sample graphs from the DIFFEQ, 3D VIEWS program, with a three-dimensional representation of a sample solution to the system of equations
$$\frac{dx}{dt} = y, \qquad \frac{dy}{dt} = -x, \qquad \text{and} \qquad \frac{dz}{dt} = 1.$$

How It Works

The program DIFFEQ, 3D VIEWS starts with a dialog box and a default xyz system. If you want an xyt system, click on the button to ‌Switch System‌. Then you enter the functions f, g, and h. In the case of xyz, be sure the functions you enter depend only on x, y, z, and not on t. See Section 5, **General Overview**, for more information about entering functions, and for features common to all programs.

The 3-space window on the left of the screen shows the x, y, and z axes and the trajectories that you have drawn.

A small plane at the top right of the screen represents either the xy-, the yz-, or the xy-plane, as chosen by the scroll bar on this little window. Any drawing done in 3-space gets projected onto these three planar views. The scroll bar lets you choose which 2D view to appear on screen. See the sample graph on the previous page.

The Information window at the lower right of the screen shows you several things:

- The range on each axis runs from -5 to 5 initially. It can be changed, however, by first clicking in the text boxes and entering the new bounds, and then clicking the ‌Set Bounds‌ button just above the text boxes. Changes are reflected in the 3-space window.
- The coordinates of the current point, the "pen", initially is located at $(0, 0, 0)$. You can change these coordinates by moving the cursor with the mouse, or clicking in the text boxes and typing in new coordinates. The ‌Solve‌ button starts drawing the solution to your system from the current pen coordinates.
- The ‌Find Sing‌ button uses the current pen position to attempt to find a singularity via Newton's method.

To Draw Trajectories

At first, the 3-space window displays only the x, y, and z axes. To draw a trajectory, either click the ‌Solve‌ button, or use the cursor alternative. You may enter an initial condition for x and y for the differential system by clicking and holding in the two-dimensional plane or the 3-space window. As you drag the mouse around in the window, several things happen:

- A dot follows the mouse in the small plane.
- The numbers in the text boxes for x, y, and z, change accordingly.
- A reference rectangle shows the current position in the 3-space window.

When the initial condition is entered, release the mouse and the program will start drawing the solution through the chosen point. The drawing proceeds first in the positive time direction and then in the negative time direction. A drawing may be stopped by clicking the mouse (don't worry about the fact that the cursor disappears while the drawing is in progress). Pressing $\boxed{\text{p}}$ while drawing pauses the program until $\boxed{\text{c}}$ is pressed. Pressing $\boxed{\text{d}}$ pauses the drawing and displays the current position of the trajectory. Again, press $\boxed{\text{c}}$ to resume drawing. You can change the approximation method or the step size under the $\boxed{\text{Change}}$ menu.

Other Features

Singularities

For an autonomous xyz system, you can find singularities, the equilibrium points where dx/dt, dy/dt, and dz/dt are all zero simultaneously. The program uses Newton's method and displays the type of singularity in the lower left corner of the Information window (the space is blank if no singularities are found). The 3-space window also draws a number at the singularity according to its type: source, sink, 2-1 saddle, or 1-2 saddle.

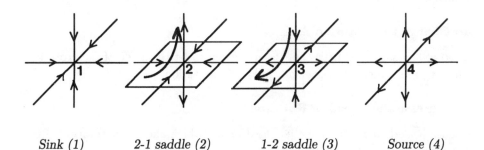

Sink (1)   *2-1 saddle (2)*   *1-2 saddle (3)*   *Source (4)*

The Information window displays only the last singularity, but the 3-space window shows all singularities found. To print a list of all found singularities, choose $\boxed{\text{Print Singularities}}$, under the $\boxed{\text{File}}$ menu. For an xyt system, the program does not find singularities, because it calculates $dt/dt = 1 \neq 0$.

To Pause After Each Point and Display the Coordinate

Choose $\boxed{\text{Pause After Each Step}}$ from the $\boxed{\text{Settings}}$ menu to stop at each new point of the trajectory and display the coordinates of the point in the Information window. The program will also draw a box at that point in 3-space so you can follow the trajectory more easily. Press the space bar to go to the next point. The space bar can be held down for continuous motion.

To Print a Numerical Listing of Points

Choose $\boxed{\text{Print Last Trajectory}}$, under the $\boxed{\text{File}}$ menu, which gives numerical listing of points for the last approximate solution. It can be used in conjunction with $\boxed{\text{Erase Last Trajectory}}$ to get a numerical printout of any trajectory.

To Zoom in on a 3D Drawing

Choose Move Towards/Away from Graph from the Tasks menu. (Notice the command key options ⌘ − and ⌘ + .)

To Rotate the Trajectories in 3D

Choose Pitch, Yaw, or Roll from the Tasks menu to rotate the graph in 3-space. The rotation axes are based on the screen, not on the x, y, and z axes in coordinate space. The 1-axis is running horizontally in the plane of the screen. The 2-axis is running vertically in the plane of the screen. The 3-axis is perpendicular to the plane of the screen.

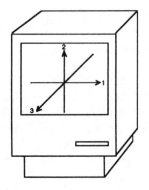

To rotate continuously use the ⌘ operations: keep ⌘ 1 pressed down to rotate around the 1-axis, and so on.

To Change the Rotation Angle

Choose Rotation Angle from the Change menu to set the angle of each rotation. The larger the angle the faster but jerkier the rotation.

To Increase the Speed of Rotation

Choose Quick rotate from the Settings menu, which allows the rotation of the 3-space trajectories to speed up. Note: it does this by drawing every third point, so the result looks less smooth.

To Rock the Graph

Choose Rock Graph from the Tasks menu. This option draws successively rotated 3D pictures, until the mouse is clicked or the machine runs out of memory. Then the graph rotates smoothly back and forth on the screen until the mouse is clicked again.

To Align 3D Graph with the xy-, yz- or xz-Plane

Choose Rotate to xy-plane, etc., from the Tasks menu to automatically align the 3D graph with two of the coordinate axes.

To Only Draw the Points of the Trajectory

Choose Draw Points Only from the Options menu to draw each trajectory as a sequence of points, not a continuous line. This option is useful when looking for the "speed" of a particle moving along that trajectory.

To Arrange the Graphs on the Printed Page

Choose $\boxed{\text{Page Layout}}$ from the $\boxed{\text{File}}$ menu. Check by the name of the graph to add it to page; click again to remove it. The layout rectangles can be dragged around, or resized, as a window. The $\boxed{\text{Square Box}}$ option makes every rectangle a square.

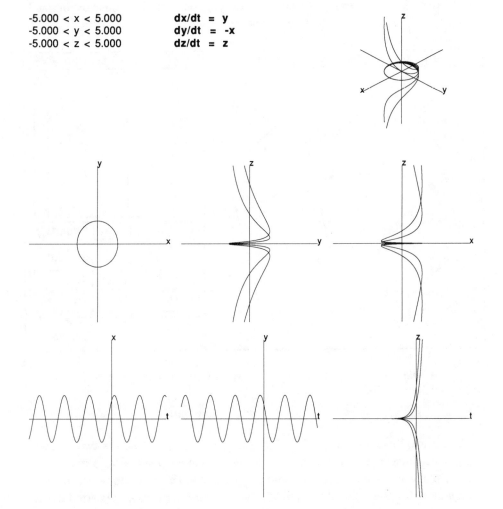

-5.000 < x < 5.000 $dx/dt = y$
-5.000 < y < 5.000 $dy/dt = -x$
-5.000 < z < 5.000 $dz/dt = z$

```
    Solutions in forward time
(x,y,z,t)
(-1.762,0.000,3.247,0.000)
(-1.753,0.176,3.347,0.100)
(-1.727,0.350,3.447,0.200)
   .
   .
   .
```

Sample Printouts from DiffEq, 3D Views. *(The coordinates list of a trajectory is a separate printout.)*

2D Periodic Equations

If you have entered xyt equations of the form

$$\frac{dx}{dt} = f(x, y, t), \qquad \frac{dy}{dt} = g(x, y, t),$$

where the functions f and g are periodic with respect to t (but not necessarily periodic with respect to either x or y), you can click the box marked $\boxed{\text{Periodic Equations}}$ in order to analyze the periodicity.

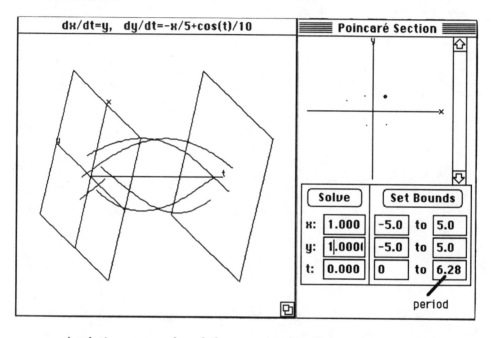

A solution, wrapped, and the corresponding Poincaré section, for

$$\frac{dx}{dt} = y, \qquad \frac{dy}{dt} = -\frac{x}{5} + \frac{\cos(t)}{10}.$$

The three-dimensional graph, on the left, in txy-space, shows two slanted xy-planes connected by a t-axis. The leftmost slanted plane always represents the xy-plane at $t = 0$. The second plane is parallel to the first and represents the xy-plane at $t =$ the value of the period, that you enter either as the period in the original function entry dialog box or as the last set of bounds in the Information window.

The second graph, on the right, shows a two-dimensional slice of txy-space, the xy-plane at $t = 0$. This is called a *Poincaré section* when it is used to show what happens to one solution to the differential equation.

The idea is to start a single trajectory from a point (x_0, y_0) in the initial xy-plane. Then when the trajectory hits the second xy-plane at (x_1, y_1), it is "wrapped" onto the initial plane and continued. That is, the coordinates (x_1, y_1) are used on the initial plane to start the next part of the trajectory, which ends on the second plane at (x_2, y_2); then (x_2, y_2) are used on the initial plane to start the next segment, ending on the second plane at (x_3, y_3), and so on.

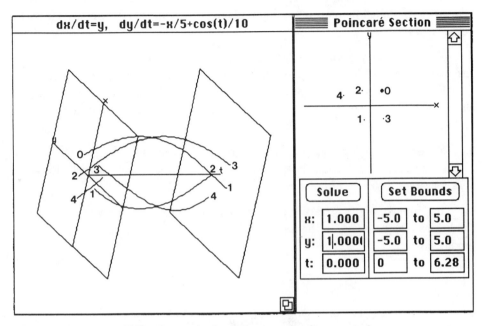

Following a single trajectory for four periods.

These points (x_0, y_0), (x_1, y_1), (x_2, y_2), ..., the Poincaré section, form an iteration pattern on the xy-plane, that can be analyzed according to methods discussed in Chapter 13 of Hubbard and West, *Differential Equations: A Dynamical Systems Approach*, Volume II.

To choose the initial condition (the point where the solution will start), click the mouse on a point in the |Poincaré Section| window or in the left-hand plane. The point's exact coordinates will appear in the |Point| window. The solution will always start at $t = 0$.

After you have selected the point, drawing proceeds in the positive time direction, as computed by the chosen method. Once the solution has reached the second slanted plane (that is, when t is equal to the presumed period), it will "jump" to the first plane again, but with the same values of x and y that hit the second plane. The solution will do that repeatedly until you click the mouse to stop drawing.

Small dots will pop up in the iteration window, corresponding to the places in the plane where the solution passes through at each period T. To stop the iteration process just click the mouse.

Some Examples to Explore

Try DIFFEQ, 3D VIEWS on the following:

1. Try the default equation $dx/dt = y$, $dy/dt = -x$ for the two-dimensional (t, x, y) case, though increasing the t bounds to show a more tightly coiled three-dimensional view.

2. Van der Pol's equation $x'' + (x^2 - 1)x' + x = 0$ describes a nonlinear electric circuit with interesting phase plane behavior described in Experiment 7 under DIFFEQ, PHASE PLANE. The three-dimensional picture is also interesting, especially when it runs backward in time. Enter this equation as a two-dimensional system $dx/dt = y$, $dy/dt = (1 - x^2)y - x$, and increase the bounds on t.

3. Another interesting equation to explore is $x'' = x^2 - t$, called "the first Painlevé transcendant"; it has been the subject of a great deal of research. Enter it as a system $dx/dt = y$, $dy/dt = t - x^2$.

4. The famous Lorenz attractor that first showed extreme sensitivity to initial conditions may be given by the following system of equations modeling weather prediction:

$$\frac{dx}{dt} = 10(y - x) ,$$

$$\frac{dy}{dt} = 28x - y - xz ,$$

$$\frac{dz}{dt} = -2.67x + xy .$$

You will need to

  (a) change the bounds to $-25 < x < 35$, $-30 < y < 35$, $-10 < z < 70$,
  (b) change the step size to something more like 0.01,
  (c) start your trajectory near the origin.

Choose Print Graph so that you can also see the xt, yt, and zt graphs (which don't show on the screen, but if you choose them under Page Layout ... you'll have them on the printout). Two of these graphs show a surprising similarity.

5. Another strange attractor in three-dimensional space is named for Rossler, and is derived from a physical situation of a dripping faucet.

$$\frac{dx}{dt} = -y - z ,$$

$$\frac{dy}{dt} = x + 0.2y ,$$

$$\frac{dz}{dt} = -5.7z + xz + 0.2 .$$

As in the previous experiment, you will need to change the bounds and step size, and you will probably want to print the graphs so that you can also see the xt, yt, and zt views. You may have to go to $\boxed{\text{Page Layout } \ldots}$ to get them on your printout.

6.   To explore the 2D PERIODIC EQUATIONS option, try a forced oscillator equation like $x'' - x' + x = \sin t$, or $dx/dt = y$, $dy/dt = y - x + \sin t$.

7.   To further explore the 2D PERIODIC EQUATIONS option, go back to the first experiment, the Van der Pol equation. See what happens when you add a forcing term like $\sin t$.

11

1D Periodic Equations

This program analyzes the behavior of the solutions to a differential equation of the form $dx/dt = f(x,t)$, where the function f is periodic with respect to t (not necessarily periodic with respect to x).

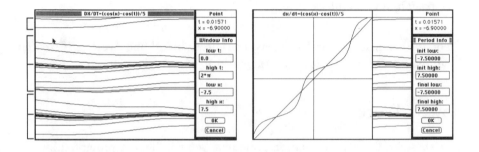

Solution Graph   Period Mapping   Remnant of
Window   Graph   Solution Graph

*Sample graphs showing wrapped solutions as well as the period mapping,
from the* 1D PERIODIC EQUATIONS, *for*

$$\frac{dx}{dt} = (\cos x - \cos t)/5 \ .$$

Solutions to the differential equation are drawn wrapped over a domain equal to one period. The solutions, by default, are computed by the Runge-Kutta method, starting from the initial condition at the beginning of the period. This is shown (for five different solutions, each bracketed in the illustration) in the solutions graph in the first window. Notice that although the differential equation is periodic in t, an individual solution is in general not periodic over the given domain.

Analysis of the situation is assisted by the second period mapping graph, which is constructed as follows: Each possible initial x_i along the left of the first graph is plotted versus the final x_f reached at the right of the first graph by the solution from that initial x_i. Whenever $x_i = x_f$, the solution $x = u(t)$ to the differential equation is periodic. These points where $x_i = x_f$ are on the diagonal of the second graph, and they are precisely the fixed points for iteration of $x_f = f(x_i)$. For example, the equation pictured has four periodic solutions in the given x-interval.

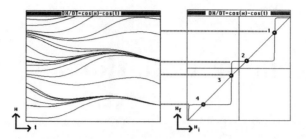

The correspondences between the two graphs: points 1 and 3 are repelling fixed points, representing unstable equilibria in the phase plane; points 2 and 4 are attracting fixed points representing stable equilibria in the phase plane.

For further mathematical analysis, consult Hubbard and West, *Differential Equations: A Dynamical Systems Approach*, Volume I, Chapter 5.5.

How It Works

As with other differential equation programs, you will be first prompted by

$$\frac{dx}{dt} =$$

for a function in x and t, where the function is periodic with respect to t. Refer to Section 5, **General Overview**, for further information on entering equations and on features common to all programs.

After you type in the equation you will be in the Graph window. You can select a slope field, in the same way as in the DIFFEQ program. To draw a trajectory, merely click anywhere in the drawing window. A trajectory will start at the leftmost side of the window at the selected x value (remember, this is the xt-plane, with the x axis being the vertical axis), continue through until the other side, wrap back around to the left, and go across the window once again. If you graph a few solutions, you will see that there are paths that trajectories are attracted to (corresponding to points 2 and 4) and those that trajectories are repelled from (corresponding to points 1 and 3). If you hit either of these paths exactly, the resultant trajectory will end up at the same x value that it started at.

To see the period mapping graph, choose $\boxed{\text{Period Mapping}}$ under the $\boxed{\text{Tasks}}$ menu. Notice that some of the right side of the Graph window is still visible to the right side of the period mapping window. The period mapping constructs the graph of the functions $x_f = f(x_i)$ where x_i is the initial value of x and x_f the final value of x after one period.

Solutions over one period
dx/dt = (cos(x)-cos(t))/5
-7.500 < x < 7.500
0.000 < t < 6.283

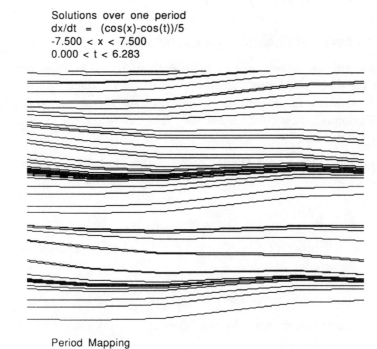

Period Mapping
-7.500 < initial x < 7.500
-7.500 < final x < 7.500

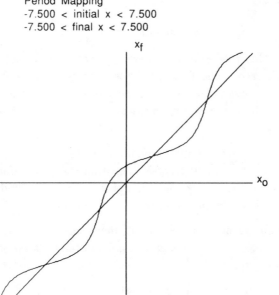

Sample printout from 1D PERIODIC EQUATIONS.

Some Examples to Explore

Try 1D PERIODIC EQUATIONS **on the following:**

1.   Play with the default example in order to appreciate this program. You can
see in the phase plane two attractive periodic cycles; there exist two repelling
periodic solutions in between them. How do these correspond to points on the
period mapping? How do the attractive cycles differ from the repelling cycles in
the period mapping?

2.   Try the following equations, both in the phase plane and the period
mapping:

$$\frac{dx}{dt} = \cos x + 1 ,$$

$$\frac{dx}{dt} = \cos x + 2 ,$$

$$\frac{dx}{dt} = \cos x - 1 .$$

Compare your results to see the effects of changing the last constant.

3.   Try phase plane drawings for the following model of population growth, first
with $a = 1$, then $a = 2$:

$$\frac{dx}{dt} = (2 + \cos t)\, x - 0.5\, x^2 - a .$$

An explanation of this model is as follows: x represents a population, and
dx/dt is its growth rate.   The factor $2 + \cos t$ represents a seasonal fertility
rate, the x^2 term represents the deleterious effect of competition or crowding
on the growth rate; the parameter a represents another negative influence due
to hunting or fishing.

   As you can see from your pictures, one case gives two possible periodic solutions (one attracting, one repelling), while the other has no periodic solutions
at all.   Experiment with changing the value of a to find the dividing value or
"bifurcation value" where the phase plane behavior changes.

   You can also experiment with the period mappings, but you will want to
change the bounds on low x to zero so as to eliminate the negative solutions that
go off to negative infinity.

   A fun thing to do with phase planes that show periodic cycles is to print out
a phase plane full of trajectories, cut it out, and wrap it into a cylinder.

12

Cascade

CASCADE shows what happens with the iteration of real quadratic polynomials of the form $x^2 + c$, as c takes on different values. A special feature of the CASCADE program is its ability to switch back and forth into an iteration routine similar to the one in ANALYZER.

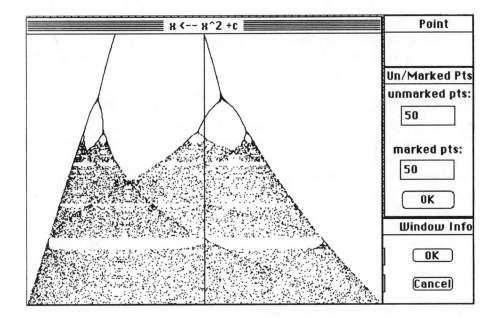

Sample screen from the CASCADE program.

Cascade of Bifurcations

CASCADE plots the c values on the vertical axis, and then goes from top to bottom plotting x on the horizontal axis, for each value of c. That is, starting at the top of the c scale, for each value of c the program will iterate $x^2 + c$ a given number of times. On each horizontal line corresponding to a given c value, dots appear showing the iterates in x. When fewer dots appear than the number of iterates for a given line, certain iterates coincide or are out of the picture. If only one dot appears on a given horizontal line, the iteration has landed on a fixed point; if only two dots appear on a given horizontal line, the iteration has landed on a cycle of period two. When a branch of the cascade splits as c gets lower, the behavior is said to bifurcate. When the dots mrege into no pattern on a line, as at the bottom ot the cascade, the orbit is *chaotic*.

For detailed discussion of the mathematics of iteration and bifurcation, see Hubbard and West, *Differential Equations: A Dynamical Systems Approach*, Volume I, Chapter 5, especially sections 5.2 and 5.3.

How It Works

To get the cascade going, choose [Iterate Cascade from Start] from the [Tasks] menu. This will fit 200 values of c along the visible vertical axis. For each value of c, from the top down, the program will iterate $x^2 + c$ a total of $k + l$ times, starting at $x = 0$; the first k iterates are *unmarked* (to clear out clutter or "noise" at the beginning of an orbit), and the next l iterates are then *marked* on the graph. You can change these numbers k and l using the the [Un/Marked Pts] window. CASCADE will discard the first k (unmarked) iterates, and plot horizontally in the x-direction the next l (marked) iterates. The idea in discarding the first k iterates is that, if the sequence is going to settle down to some particular behavior, we hope it will have done so after k iterates. In practice, $k = 50$ is adequate for large-scale pictures, but blowups require larger values of k and l. Larger k makes for cleaner pictures at any stage. Larger l gives more dots on every line. The picture on the previous page was made with $k = 50$ and $l = 50$.

Features

To Analyze by the Iteration Routine

The program switches back and forth with the ability to iterate any n-th iterate for any given value of c, as illustrated on the opposite page. Choose the c for the iteration either numerically (choose [Analyze at a Value] from the [Tasks] menu) or by clicking on the cascade graph (choose [Analyze at a Click] from the [Tasks] menu). Furthermore, you can do the iteration on whichever iterate of your function you choose. For example, if you wish to analyze the fifth iterate, change the iterate number (in the N-th Iterate window) from 1 to 5.

To Change the Equation

CASCADE is provided with only the two equations that are discussed in Hubbard and West, *Differential Equations: A Dynamical Systems Approach*, Volume I, Chapter 5. That is, it studies either the real quadratic function $x^2 + c$, or Newton's method for the cubic polynomial $f(x) = x^3 + cx + 1$, which is

$$x - \frac{f(x)}{f'(x)} \quad \text{or} \quad \frac{2x^3 - 1}{3x^2 + c} \, .$$

You can change the equation by choosing the appropriate option from the Change menu. The amazing fact is that these two very different functions yield essentially the same cascade picture, though at very different scales.

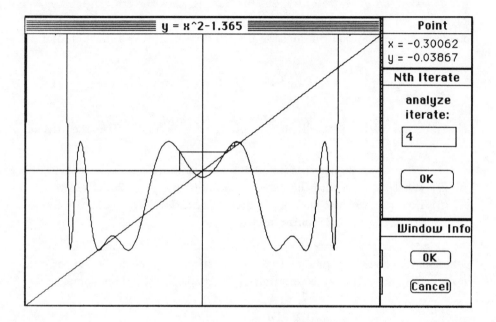

Sample analyzing screen from CASCADE.

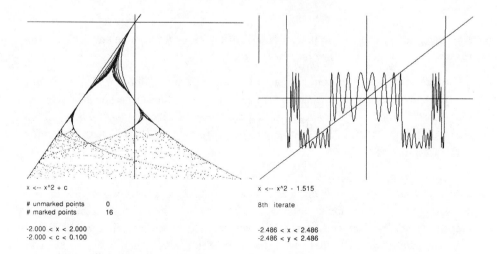

Sample printouts from CASCADE.

Some Examples to Explore

Try CASCADE on the following:

Experiments #1–7 use the quadratic equation $x^2 + c$; experiments #8–11 use
Newton's method for the cubic equation $x^3 + cx + 1 = 0$.

1. *The skeleton of the cascade.* The program iterates the critical point $x = 0$
for varying values of c. Try setting the unmarked points to 0, and the marked
points to 16, so that you consider the first 16 iterates of 0 as a function of c:

$$c, \quad c^2 + c, \quad \left(c^2 + c\right)^2 + c, \quad \left(\left(c^2 + c\right)^2 + c\right)^2 + c, \quad \text{etc.}$$

The program CASCADE will now graph these functions. Use the domain
$-3 \le c \le 1$.

   (1) What happens with the iterates when c is above 1/4, or below -2?
   (2) What happens with the iterates when c is between -2 and 1/4?
   (3) How can you use such a picture to locate attracting cycles? Super-
       attracting cycles? Neutral cycles?

2. *Windows in the cascade.* Draw the cascade with, for example, 30 unmarked
points and 30 marked points (so that the iterations have been allowed to settle
down on any attracting cycle or strange attractor). Use the three domains:

$$
\begin{aligned}
&\text{(a)} && -2 \quad\;\, \le c \le -1.75\,, \\
&\text{(b)} && -1.75 \le c \le -1.5\,, \\
&\text{(c)} && -1.5 \quad\, \le c \le -1.25\,.
\end{aligned}
$$

Raise the number of points per pixel to 10 (if you have patience enough!) to see
the window structure somewhat more clearly.

Locate attracting cycles in the cascade. For each cycle (of order n) you should
analyze the cycle choosing ⏐Analyze Step by Step⏐ to produce the associated cobweb
diagram of the cycle. You should also graph the n-th iterate (corresponding to
the order of the cycle). Note whether there are other nonattracting cycles for
that particular value of c.

3. *Shadows in the cascade.* The cascade is filled with masses of dots within
which you can see clearly marked shadows. What happens when one of the
shadows passes through the critical value 0? How are the shadows related to the
graphs of the first few iterations of the critical point (see experiment 1)? What
happens where two such shadows cross each other? Use ⏐Analyze Step by Step⏐ at
the corresponding c values.

4. *Superattracting cycles.* Use ANALYZER to graph the first five iterations of the critical point:

$$c, \quad c^2 + c, \quad \left(c^2 + c\right)^2 + c, \quad \left(\left(c^2 + c\right)^2 + c\right)^2 + c, \quad \left(\left(\left(c^2 + c\right)^2 + c\right)^2 + c\right)^2 + c.$$

You will need to enter and graph these expressions as functions of x! Locate the roots of these functions. That will give you a catalogue of superattracting cycles of orders 1 to 5. Use CASCADE to $\boxed{\text{Analyze Step by Step}}$ at these particular c values so you can produce the associated cobweb diagrams.

(1) Note the c value for the first appearance of cycles of each order 1, 2, 3, 4, and 5.

(2) Note the c values for the last appearance of cycles of each order 1, 2, 3, 4, and 5.

(3) In what order of c values do the cycles make their first appearance? Their last appearance? Make a conjecture for the cycles of order 6, and check it!

(4) What does the cobweb diagram look like for the last appearing cycle of order n in the cascade?

5. *Bifurcations.* Locate the two attracting 4-cycles (cycles of order four) in the cascade. Analyze the graph of the fourth iterate before, during and after the 4-cycle was attracting. Describe the creation of the attracting 4-cycle in the two cases. Do the same with the 2-cycle and the 3-cycle.

6. *Misiurewicz points.* The dot pattern of the cascade has several branching points where disconnected pieces of the attractor merge. Locate such branching points, and analyze the iterations of 0 for such a particular value of c. Describe the behavior of the critical point $x = 0$ under iteration.

Do the same for one of the points within the cascade, where several shadow lines cross each other. (It is most easy to locate such points when you only graph the first 8, say, iterates of the critical points; see experiment 1.)

7. *The Feigenbaum point.* The main branch $(-3/4 \leq c \leq 1/4)$ of the cascade splits into two subbranches, which themselves split into two subbranches, etc.; the period doubling of the cascade. Use the cascade to blow up and locate the c values corresponding to the superattracting 2-, 4-, 8-, 16-, ... -cycles in the period doubling. Show that these c values converge geometrically towards a limiting value where chaos reigns. Estimate the rate of convergence (the first Feigenbaum parameter) as well as the limiting value (the Feigenbaum point).

8.   *Newton's method for a cubic.* Use ANALYZER to graph the cubic polynomial $x^3 + cx + 1$ for the following eight values of c:

$$c \ = \ 1, \quad 0.5, \quad 0, \quad -0.5, \quad -1, \quad -1.5, \quad -2, \quad -2.5.$$

Note the number of real roots, and their (approximate) positions, for each of these c values. Try also to find the roots using Newton's method with the inflection point $x = 0$ (or as close as you can get to it) as the starting point.

9.   *The failure of Newton's method to converge to a root.* Use CASCADE to graph the bifurcation diagram for Newton's method for a cubic using the domain $-3 \le c \le 1$. Use 30 unmarked points and 15 marked points to give Newton's method a chance to stabilize at a root. If you have patience enough, it may clarifiy the diagram to raise the number of steps per pixel to 10.

   Where do the main branches in the bifurcation diagram come from? What goes wrong at $c = 0$? For what c values do you get mini-cascades? (You may blow up some of the promising "blobs" to see if they really are mini-cascades!) What goes wrong at a mini-cascade?

   You might also try to calculate for yourself the particular c value for which the critical point $x = 0$ returns to itself after two iterations, as well as the particular values of c for which the critical point $x = 0$ iterates to infinity after two iterations, and compare your results with your graphical findings above.

10.   *Cycling in Newton's method for a cubic.* Use CASCADE to graph the bifurcation diagram for Newton's method for a cubic, using the domain $-2 \le c \le 0$. Analyze the iteration at some c values for which there is a superattracting cycle (characterized by a crossing at the critical point $x = 0$). Use the critical point $x = 0$ as a starting point for iterating the rational function

$$\frac{2x^3 - 1}{3x^2 + c}.$$

What happens to it under iteration? Compare with the graph of the n-th iterate, where n is the period of the attracting cycle. You might continue this investigation, using the ANALYZER program, by rootfinding in the cubic polynomial $x^3 + cx + 1$ using Newton's method with the starting point $x = 0$.

11.   *Universality of the cascade.* Use CASCADE to graph the bifurcation diagram for Newton's method for a cubic using the domain $-2 \le c \le 0$. Blow up a mini-cascade, and compare its structure with that coming from the quadratic iterations. What happens to the main branch? Can you locate similar windows? Try answering other questions that occur to you.

13

2D Iterations

For a system of two equations of the form:

$$x = f(x, y), \qquad y = g(x, y)$$

and a given seed or initial point (x_0, y_0), this program plots the orbit under iteration. That is, it plots the sequence of points (x_0, y_0), (x_1, y_1), (x_2, y_2), $(x_3, y_3), \ldots$, where

$$
\begin{aligned}
x_1 &= f(x_0, y_0), & y_1 &= g(x_0, y_0), \\
x_2 &= f(x_1, y_1), & y_2 &= g(x_1, y_1), \\
x_3 &= f(x_2, y_2), & y_3 &= g(x_2, y_2) \quad \ldots
\end{aligned}
$$

Iteration is discussed in Section 3, **Iteration**, of this manual. A more thorough treatment of iteration in two dimensions appears in Chapter 13 of Hubbard and West, *Differential Equations: A Dynamical Systems Approach*, Volume II.

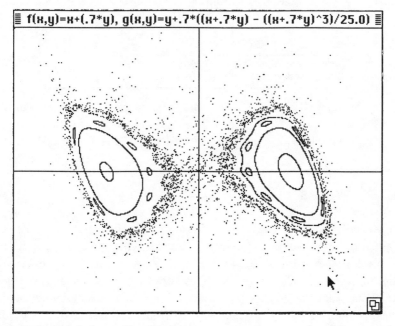

Sample graph from the 2D ITERATIONS program, showing several orbits, for the system of equations

$$f(x, y) = x + 0.7y, \qquad g(x, y) = y + 0.7\left\{ (x + 0.7y) - (x + 0.7y)^3 / 25 \right\}.$$

The orbits behave in ways similar to differential equations. They have singularities called sinks, sources, and saddles; however, all the singularities are of three types: regular, flip, or double flip. See Section 3, **Iteration**, for more information.

The program also draws the separatrices for the saddles it finds. First it draws the unstable ones (forward iterates in one eigendirection), then, if the inverses of the equations have been entered, the stable ones (backwards iterates in the other eigendirection). Unlike the case of differential equations, here the separatrices of the saddle point can cross, which they do zillions of times. To help sort out the confusion, the unstable separatrix is in black while the stable separatrix is dotted.

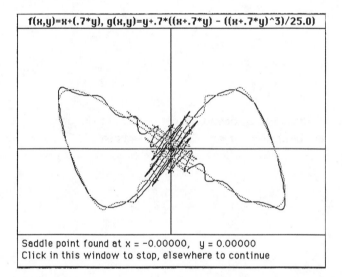

Stable (dotted) and unstable (black) separatrices for the system of equations

$$f(x,y) = x + 0.7y, \qquad g(x,y) = y + 0.7 \left\{ (x + 0.7y) - (x + 0.7y)^3 / 25 \right\}.$$

How It Works

First, you will be asked to type in an iteration equation, or go with the default. The program also asks for the inverse functions, which you can type in, or just leave blank if they do not exist or you don't know them. If you press Return or click on OK, just click anywhere in the drawing window to iterate from that point. Each iteration itself is just a sequence of points, sometimes making an interesting path or pattern. Click again to halt the iteration. You can now pick another starting point to iterate to get a better idea of what the function is doing. Notice that on a color screen different orbits will be represented by different colors.

If a particular area looks more interesting you can take a closer look using
Blow Up from the Task menu (see Section 5, **General Overview**, for instructions).

Other Features

To Locate a Singularity

A singularity is a fixed point, or more generally a periodic point. The program
will look for periodic points of the last determined or chosen period. Check the
period with Enter New Period (select Period under the Change menu).

Choose Locate Singularity from the Tasks menu and click on the drawing
window near where you think a singularity could be. This option will also draw
the separatrices of a saddle point. If the inverse functions are not specified,
then the stable separatrices (the backward ones) will not be drawn. For periodic
points with high order the separatrices may appear so ragged as to be false.

Click the mouse inside the window at the bottom to exit the mode.

To Change the Color of an Orbit

The default setting is Cycle Color, where you will cycle through the six colors:
black, magenta, blue, red, green, cyan in the order indicated. You can also just
select the color of the next orbit and keep cycling from that color. If you remove
the check mark on the Cycle Color, the color will be fixed.

To Change Equations, Tolerance for Periodic Points

Choose the appropriate option from the Change menu. When locating a singularity (i.e., a periodic point) the program uses Newton's method. The tolerance
specifies how close to the singularity you should be before the Newton's iterations
should stop.

To Find the Period of the Function

Choose Period from the Tasks menu. Then surround the suspected periodic
point by a small box by dragging the mouse across the periodic point. A dialog
box pops up: Start iteration in the center?. Click OK and the program will check
after how many iterations the center point will return to the box. The period
determined this way will be listed in the Point window.

To Enter a New Period of the Function

Choose Enter New Period from the Tasks menu. A dialog box pops up which
presents you with the last determined period as default value. If you want to

check if a given region contains periodic points of a specific period, you can enter this new period and choose ⬚Locate Singularity⬚ from the ⬚Tasks⬚ menu. In this way you can confirm the existence of periodic points.

To Print the Graph

Choose ⬚Print Graph⬚ from the ⬚File⬚ menu. The printout will include the functions and the window bounds as well as the graph; if you choose ⬚With Starting Points⬚, you'll also get a color coded list of them (in either forward or reverse order of the order in which they were selected).

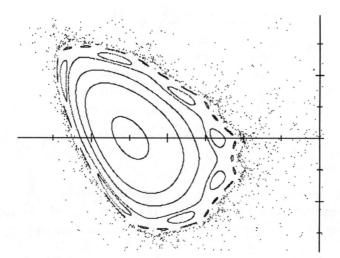

```
f=x+(.7*y)
g=y+.7*((x+.7*y)  -  ((x+.7*y)^3)/25.0)
-7.950 < x < 0.100
-3.600 < y < 3.900
             Initial  pt    # of It.
(-2.757750,-0.450000) 916
(-2.133875,-0.625000) 725
(-6.662000,-1.975000) 448
(-1.912500,0.700000)  908
(-2.315000,0.775000)  577
(-2.174125,0.825000)  938
(-4.569000,0.025000)  433
(-3.703625,0.000000)  781
(-3.341375,0.075000)  955
(-2.496125,0.000000)  1007
(-2.938875,1.025000)  2195
(-2.496125,2.825000)  2712
```

Sample printout from 2D Iterations.

Some Examples to Explore

Try 2D ITERATIONS **on the following:**

1. To understand the criss-crossed separatrices of a saddle, use the default example and locate the singularity at $(0,0)$; then watch how the separatrices grow. Each of the four paths away from $(0,0)$ makes bigger and bigger zigzags, closer and closer together; the two black ones are forward in time, and the two gray ones are backward in time. Each of the four can be stopped by a click.

The best way to test their role is to make a blowup that nearly fills the screen; you might want to move the point window to the far right and leave it exposed. Then locate the singularity again and let each of the four separatrices go only until it starts to fold back very close to itself. You will now have a picture with lots of loops divided up into regions by the crisscross. Under the Settings menu choose Display Point After Each Step ; then go to Tasks and choose Draw Orbit . A good place to begin is in the first quadrant, in your first clear little enclosed loop as you walk away from the origin, e.g., about $(1.1, 1.2)$. Start an orbit right in the middle of that loop, and observe that the next point is drawn in the middle of the next loop away from the origin. Keep drawing another point of the orbit by hitting the space bar, and see if you can predict where the images will appear – it gets particularly interesting in the crisscross regions. But it is the exact location of your starting point within the crisscross of the black first forward orbit that determines whether the orbit ends up outside or inside the basic figure eight. That is, it depends on which side of the black you are really on – then your orbit will always stay on that side. The separatrices do exactly separate the "inside" orbits from the "outside" orbits.

2. Experiment further with the default mapping, finding the periods of various chains of islands. Then look for the saddles between them. If the period of the islands is high, the drawings may get too crazy to be real.

3. Try various Henon mappings,

$$\begin{pmatrix} x \\ y \end{pmatrix} \longrightarrow \begin{pmatrix} x^2 + c - ay \\ x \end{pmatrix},$$

for various values of c and a. For instance, you might try $a = -1$ and $c = 0.5$, -2, -2.8, each of which gives a different picture. Make blowups of interesting areas and try to find the period of different orbits.

The results are so difficult to predict that this is an important area of current research in dynamical systems.

The Henon mappings can be seen as an extension of the quadratic map $x^2 + c$, but quickly become far more complicated for $a \neq 0$. One reason for this is that they are *invertible*, for $a \neq 0$, with inverse map

$$\begin{pmatrix} x \\ y \end{pmatrix} \longrightarrow \begin{pmatrix} y \\ (y^2 + c - x)/a \end{pmatrix} .$$

If you type in these inverse functions, you'll be able to locate saddles and draw the separatrices between islands. If the period of the islands is high, the drawings may get too crazy to be real.

4.   You might try some of the various mappings due to Barry Martin, of Birmingham, England. Two of the possibilities are

$$\begin{pmatrix} x \\ y \end{pmatrix} \longrightarrow \begin{pmatrix} y - \sin x \\ a - x \end{pmatrix}$$

or

$$\begin{pmatrix} x \\ y \end{pmatrix} \longrightarrow \begin{pmatrix} y - \text{sign}\,(x) * \sqrt{|bx - c|} \\ a - x \end{pmatrix} .$$

These give an entirely different sort of picture, and are much less understood than Henon mappings. These Martin mappings are the topic of an interesting article "Wallpaper for the Mind" by A. K. Dewdney in *Scientific American*, September, 1986. There we can see some of the patterns, and we are told that a most interesting series of patterns occurs by the first formula when a lies within 0.7 of π. If any pattern at first glance looks thick and dull, you might try blowing up to get more of the fine detail. Suggested values for (a, b, c) in the second formula are

$(-200, 0.1, -80)$
$(0.4, 1, 0)$
$(-\pi, 0.3, 0.3)$ different from $(-3.14, 0.3, 0.3)$?

5.   Look at Experiment #6 in Section 9, **Diffeq, Phase Plane**, for the differential equation of a double well potential. The trajectories in that example are approximated by a modified Euler method to produce the default example for 2D Iterations.

$$\frac{dx}{dt} = y \qquad \text{is replaced by} \qquad x_{n+1} = x_n + h\,y_n ,$$

$$\frac{dy}{dt} = -V'(x) \qquad \text{is replaced by} \qquad y_{n+1} = y_n - h\,V'(x_{n+1}) .$$

The use of x_{n+1} on the right makes the iteration *area-preserving* and *invertible*. Thus we have

$$\begin{aligned} y_n &= y_{n+1} + h\,V'(x_{n+1}) , \\ x_n &= x_{n+1} - h\,y_n . \end{aligned}$$

With a stepsize $h = 0.7$, the chaotic picture results.

You might notice especially the phenomenon of "numerical tunneling". In the differential equation, the potential $V(x)$ looks like ; a particle starting in one well cannot penetrate into the other well, due to a lack of extra energy. But with iterations, energy is no longer strictly conserved, and that allows the particle to penetrate the barrier anyway. Try, for example, the starting point $(1, 0)$ in the right-hand well, and use Display Point After Each Step to follow the orbit closely enough to see when and how the tunneling to the left begins.

Let's return to observing how the chaos develops. Try a smaller stepsize, for example $h = 0.1$, to see trajectories that look very much like those for the differential equation. As h increases, you can watch the chaos creep in.

In fact, the "chaos" is always there if you look at a sufficiently large portion of the plane. On a graph window with $-50 \leq x \leq 50$, $-37.5 \leq y \leq 37.5$, try $h = 0.1$, then clear the screen and try $h = 0.3$, then $h = 0.5$. Can you conjecture what pattern seems to evolve as you use larger stepsizes h?

6. The dynamics of complex numbers $z = x + iy$ can be studied by iteration in two dimensions. For studying the famous Julia sets for $z^2 + c$, where $c = a + ib$ is also a complex number, simply enter

$$f(x, y) = x^2 - y^2 + a, \qquad g(x, y) = 2xy + b.$$

One source of interesting values of c is the cardioid boundary of the body of the Mandelbrot set. Those satisfy the equation

$$c \quad = \quad \left(\tfrac{1}{2}(1 - \cos 2\pi t)\cos 2\pi t + \tfrac{1}{4}\right) + i\left(\tfrac{1}{2}(1 - \cos 2\pi t)\sin 2\pi t\right)$$

for t the *rotation number*, the fraction of a full rotation (about the cusp of the cardioid).

For rational rotation number t, you will see orbits that give a "flower structure", showing periodicity of orbits in the ball attached at that point.

For irrational rotation number t, you will see orbits that give "Siegel disks" as the orbit of $(0, 0)$ and nested closed curves inside. All other orbits that begin outside the Siegel disk are either attracted to those on or inside the Siegel disk, or they escape to infinity.

7. This program can be used to draw CASCADE pictures for *arbitrary* real functions with a single parameter, using the y value as the parameter. For example, try

$$f(x,y) = yx(1-x), \quad g(x,y) = y + 0.00004, \quad \text{with} \quad 0 < x < 1, \quad 3.5 < y < 4.$$

Start with $(x_0, y_0) = (0, 3.5)$, at the lower left corner of the screen. The extra 0.000004 in the y value is what makes the orbit creep up the graph. This "creep constant" is calculated approximately as

$$\frac{y\text{-interval}}{\left(\begin{array}{c} 300 \text{ pixels on} \\ \text{vertical axis} \end{array} \right) \left(\begin{array}{c} \text{number of horizontal} \\ \text{marked points desired} \\ \text{for each vertical pixel} \end{array} \right)} .$$

14

EigenFinder

This program finds the eigenvalues λ and eigenvectors $\mathbf{v}$ of a matrix A, of size up to 12×12. That is, EIGENFINDER finds λ and $\mathbf{v}$ such that $A\mathbf{v} = \lambda\mathbf{v}$. The process of finding the eigenvalues is called *diagonalization* of the matrix, because the final result is an eigenvalue matrix, A^*, with the eigenvalues lying along the main diagonal and zeros elsewhere. This diagonal matrix, A^*, has the same eigenvalues and determinant and trace as the original matrix, A.

Two methods, Jacobi's method and the QR Algorithm, are available in the program. Jacobi's method is the faster of the two but only works with symmetric matrices. The QR algorithm can handle the nonsymmetric ones, but it is slower and requires more iterations to find the eigenvalues that have the same precision as under Jacobi's method. For a detailed description of these two algorithms, see Hubbard and West, *Differential Equations: A Dynamical Systems Approach*, Volume II, Appendix L6-L8.

Sample displays from the EIGENFINDER *program.*

How It Works

EIGENFINDER starts by prompting you for the matrix. Originally the matrix size is set to 12×12, but you may change that by using the Change Size button.

To fill the matrix, type numbers in each entry box. You can either click on the desired box or tab between them. A box that does not contain a number will be assigned a value of zero. Some other shortcuts include Symmetrize (symmetrize upper off-diagonal elements with lower off-diagonal elements), Repeat First Row & Column Along Diagonal, and Fill by Formula.

Fill by Formula will accept a formula in terms of the indices i and j.

Once your matrix is filled, click OK. Now you are ready to find the eigenvalues and eigenvectors.

Select either Jacobi's Method or QR Algorithm on the Settings menu. Remember that Jacobi's method only works if matrices are symmetric (the program will remind you if you forget). The Settings menu also allows you to choose whether you want the program to display, pause, and/or print automatically after each iteration. Use the Tasks menu to start the iteration.

Jacobi's method shows its progress as it iterates, and continues iterating until the largest off-diagonal element is less than the tolerance. The tolerance is initially set to be 10^{-4}, but you may change it by using the Tolerance option on the Change menu. The smallest tolerance accepted is 10^{-8}; any smaller entry will be limited to this value.

The QR algorithm uses quadratic convergence to get diagonal elements that are real eigenvalues, or 2×2 matrices along the diagonal giving complex eigenvalues. The goal is to get zeros below these diagonal elements; the algorithm stops when no lower off-diagonal elements exceed the tolerance.

To Find Eigenvalues and Eigenvectors

Eigenvalues displays both real and complex eigenvalues, to the number of digits selected under Tolerance. Real eigenvalues, to fewer decimal places, are displayed along the diagonal of the final iterated matrix. Complex pairs of eigenvalues are found from 2×2 "boxes" along the diagonal; in each case, the complex eigenvalues are found from computing the characteristic polynomial for just those 2×2 "boxes". Although each "box" changes on each iteration, you will find that the characteristic polynomial indeed stabilizes.

Eigenvectors can be displayed at any time with Jacobi's method; but with the QR algorithm, the eigenvectors do not arise as a by-product and are not available immediately after the eigenvalues have been found, so you must use the Tasks menu. The Find Eigenvectors item, which appears only if the QR algorithm finds the eigenvalues and stops itself after having reached the tolerance, starts a simple row reduction, back substitution algorithm which finds the eigenvectors.

> **DONE! Number of iterations: 16**
> **All lower off-diagonal elements are less than 0.0001**
> Display...   ⦿ Whole matrix   ○ Eigenvalues   [PRINT]
>
> Final MATRIX
>
> | 7.25882 | -4.8876 | -7.1111 | -3.7847 |
> | 4.13761 | 9.85501 | 7.02645 | 3.95570 |
> | 0.00000 | 0.00007 | 5.42403 | 1.27822 |
> | 0.00000 | 0.00000 | 0.00000 | 0.46212 |

> **DONE! Number of iterations: 16**
> **All lower off-diagonal elements are less than 0.0001**
> Display...   ○ Whole matrix   ⦿ Eigenvalues   [PRINT]
>
> Tolerance: 0.0001
>
> Final EIGENVALUES
>
> 8.5569+4.3056i
> 8.5569-4.3056i
> 5.4240
> 0.4621

Two more (separate) screens from the EIGENFINDER program, the bottom immediately follows the top one. As you can see, the two complex eigenvalues correspond to a two by two square on the main diagonal of the matrix.

Features

To See How the Iteration is Progressing

At any point while iteration is in progress you may click the [PAUSE] button to suspend it temporarily (use [RESUME] to continue), or you may click [ABORT] to stop it for good, in which case you will have to use the [Tasks] menu to restart the algorithm from the very beginning. You may click on [Whole Matrix] or [Eigenvalues] at any point, whether the program is paused or not, to see how any of these are coming along. If you select [Pause After Each Iteration] from the [Settings] menu beforehand, then you can see step-by-step what is going on.

The ⎡Settings⎤ menu remains active throughout processing, so you may change any of the options at any time. This is convenient if you start the algorithm with ⎡Pause ...⎤ or ⎡Print After Each Iteration⎤ active but find that they are no longer needed.

If you have chosen ⎡Print After Each Iteration⎤, the cursor disappears during printing and you may have a little difficulty getting at the ⎡Settings⎤ menu or the buttons for ⎡PAUSE⎤ or ⎡ABORT⎤. By the time you get the cursor up there you may find that it has disappeared again for the next print. Just be quick to put it over the button or menu that you want before it disappears and hold down the mouse button (you might want to click it a few times first). You will gain control once the current print is done.

The ⎡PRINT⎤ button may be used to print whatever is displayed in the window below the controls.

Original matrix:

2.00000	4.00000	-3.0000
4.00000	1.00000	3.00000
-3.0000	3.00000	1.00000

Eigenvalues and Eigenvectors:

5.5608	-5.3553	3.7945
-7.0146	1.0104	-0.3292
-5.4943	-1.1080	0.6023
1.0000	1.0000	1.0000

Original matrix:

2.00000	4.00000	-3.0000
4.00000	1.00000	3.00000
-3.0000	3.00000	1.00000

Matrix after 1 iterations:

2.10344	5.01958	-0.0000
5.01958	-1.9376	0.60306
0.00000	0.60306	3.83421

Matrix after 2 iterations:

2.24447	4.99157	0.00000
4.99157	-2.0568	0.42747
0.00000	0.42747	3.81241

Matrix after 3 iterations:

2.40050	4.93682	-0.0000
4.93682	-2.2029	0.30123
0.00000	0.30123	3.80244

Matrix after 4 iterations:

2.56028	4.86668	0.00000
4.86668	-2.3582	0.21174
0.00000	0.21174	3.79798

⋮

Sample EIGENFINDER *printouts.*

Some Examples to Explore

Try EIGENFINDER on the following:

1. Find the eigenvalues of the 2 × 2 matrices

$$\begin{pmatrix} 0 & -1 \\ 2 & 3 \end{pmatrix}, \quad \begin{pmatrix} 1 & -1 \\ 2 & 3 \end{pmatrix}$$

to check that the program really works.

Note: these matrices are not symmetric, so you must use the QR method; Jacobi's method does not apply.

2. Try the 3 × 3 matrices

$$\begin{pmatrix} 0 & 1 & 0 \\ 0 & 0 & 1 \\ 6 & -11 & 6 \end{pmatrix}, \quad \begin{pmatrix} 0 & 1 & 0 \\ 0 & 0 & 1 \\ 2 & -1 & 2 \end{pmatrix}.$$

Again, you should be able to verify by hand that the results are right.

3. Use the program on the matrix

$$\begin{pmatrix} 2 & -1 & 0 \\ -1 & 2 & -1 \\ 0 & -1 & 2 \end{pmatrix}.$$

This time the matrix is symmetric, so that you can use both Jacobi's method and the QR method, and you should check that they agree.

4. Now try both methods for the larger analogous matrices with "2" on the diagonal and "−1" above and below, for matrices of size 6, 8, 9, 10, and 12. You can enter these matrices by hand, but it is much easier to enter them as follows:

> Start with the identity matrix.

> Edit the first row and column to read 2, −1, and 0 where desired; then simply choose the option $\boxed{\text{Repeat First Row and Column along Diagonals}}$.

Again, you can use both methods, and you should look at the eigenvalues and observe the coincidences.

5. Further examples that can yield surprises are

$$a_{i,j} = \sin(i - j), \qquad a_{i,j} = \sin(i + j), \qquad a_{i,j} = \sin(i - j) + i.$$

15

JacobiDraw

This program demonstrates Jacobi's method for the diagonalization of a symmetric 3×3 matrix, that is, finding its eigenvalues. It does this both algebraically and geometrically, the latter by representing the matrix with a quadric surface and animating the effects of diagonalization on the surface.

$$\begin{pmatrix} 2 & 1 & 0 \\ 1 & 2 & 1 \\ 0 & 1 & 2 \end{pmatrix}$$

Eigenvalues
3.4, 0.6, 2.0

$$\begin{pmatrix} 2 & 1 & 0 \\ 1 & -2 & 1 \\ 0 & 1 & -2 \end{pmatrix}$$

Eigenvalues
2.25, −3.1, −1.15

$$\begin{pmatrix} 2 & 0 & 3 \\ 0 & 0 & 0 \\ 3 & 0 & -1 \end{pmatrix}$$

Eigenvalues
3.8, 0, −2.8

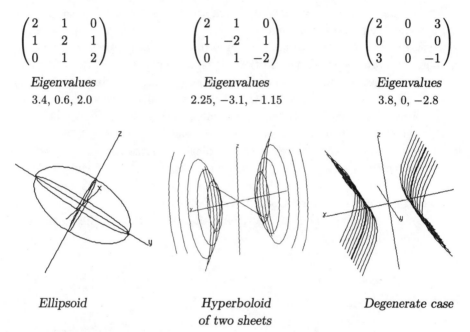

Ellipsoid

*Hyperboloid
of two sheets*

Degenerate case

Three different graphs from the JACOBIDRAW program.

The type of surface plotted depends on the eigenvalues of the matrix. If all three eigenvalues have the same sign, it will be an ellipsoid (which looks like a jelly bean, as at the left of the above figure); otherwise, it will be a hyperboloid of one sheet (which looks like the middle part of an hourglass), or a hyperboloid of two sheets (as in the center picture). If any of the eigenvalues are zero, you may end up with a cylinder or some other degenerate form (as at the right).

The dimensions of the quadric surface are related to the magnitudes of the eigenvalues. For example, if the eigenvalues are nearly equal, an ellipsoid will tend to be more spherical, if the eigenvalues are unequal, the quadratic surface will be elongated along one or more axes. These surfaces are represented by their intersections with each of the xy-, yz-, and xz-planes.

Each iteration of Jacobi's method serves to move the axis system closer to being aligned with the principal axes of the entire quadric surface. This is done by working in one plane for each iteration — the plane chosen is the one in which the surface is most out of alignment. During each iteration, the axis system rotates in this plane until it lines up with the principal axes of the ellipse or hyperbola that results from the plane's intersection with the surface. Geometrically, these planewise rotations are the meat of Jacobi's method, and each one corresponds to bringing the largest off-diagonal element of the matrix to zero. At the end of each iteration, the surface is redrawn on the newly positioned axis system.

At this point you may wonder why, if each iteration serves to align the surface in one plane, the process would not be done after three iterations — one for each of the three planes? Each rotation may undo the effects of the previous rotation, misaligning a previously aligned section. It is as trying to solve Rubik's cube, in which case getting all the same color on one side often destroys a previous triumph on another side. In the matrix, this new misalignment corresponds to a previously zeroed off-diagonal element coming back to life. Fortunately, this newly revived term will not be as large as it was before. In fact, with each iteration, the sum of the squares of the off-diagonal terms is decreased by the square of the term being zeroed, as proved in Appendix L8 of Hubbard and West, *Differential Equations: A Dynamical Systems Approach*, Volume II. Thus the matrix becomes more diagonal and eventually this sum is less than a certain predetermined tolerance, and the algorithm halts. At that point, the eigenvalues appear along the diagonal of the matrix.

How It Works

After starting the program you are prompted with $\boxed{\text{Enter Symmetric Matrix}}$. The program only shows the lower left half of the matrix, so the matrix you enter will always be symmetric. After you are satisfied, click on $\boxed{\text{OK}}$. The program automatically draws a view of the quadric surface in 3-space, and displays your matrix in the Status window.

Features

To Find Eigenvalues and Eigenvectors

Choose $\boxed{\text{Find Eigenvalues}}$ from the $\boxed{\text{Tasks}}$ menu. The program will display the eigenvalues and eigenvectors in the Status window. Choosing $\boxed{\text{Reset Matrix}}$ will return the original matrix to the Status window, and return the axis in the graph window to normal.

To Pause or Print After Each Iteration

These are located in the [Settings] menu. They are especially useful for observing how Jacobi's method corrects the plane that has the greatest error.

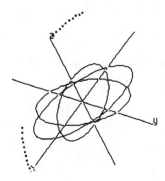

Iteration 1: Rotating -31.717 degrees in the XZ plane

Matrix during iteration 1:

$$\begin{bmatrix} 3.0000 & -1.0000 & \mathbf{2.0000} \\ -1.0000 & 2.0000 & -2.0000 \\ \mathbf{2.0000} & -2.0000 & 5.0000 \end{bmatrix}$$

$$\downarrow$$

$$\begin{bmatrix} 1.7639 & 0.2008 & \mathbf{-0.0000} \\ 0.2008 & 2.0000 & -2.2270 \\ \mathbf{-0.0000} & 2.2270 & 6.2361 \end{bmatrix}$$

Printout of one step of Jacobi's method.

To Zoom in on a 3D Drawing

Choose [Move towards/away from graph] from the [Tasks] menu or use [⌘ −] and [⌘ +] .

To Rotate the Trajectories in 3D

Choose [Pitch], [Yaw], or [Roll] from the [Tasks] menu to rotate the graph in 3-space. The rotation axes are based on the screen, not on the x-, y- and z-axes in coordinate space. The 1-axis runs horizontally in the plane of the screen. The 2-axis runs vertically in the plane of the screen. The 3-axis is perpendicular to the plane of the screen. To rotate continuously use the ⌘ operations: e.g., keep [⌘ 1] pressed down to rotate around the 1-axis.

To Change the Rotation Angle

Choose $\boxed{\text{Rotation Angle}}$ from the $\boxed{\text{Change}}$ menu to set the angle of each rotation. The larger the angle the faster but jerkier the rotation.

To Align 3D Graph With the xy-, xz-, or yz-Planes

Choose $\boxed{\text{Rotate to } xy\text{-plane}}$ from the $\boxed{\text{Tasks}}$ menu to automatically align the 3D graph with two of the coordinate axes.

To Change the Tolerance, Grid Size, or Matrix

Select the item you wish to change from the $\boxed{\text{Change}}$ menu. You will be prompted with a window displaying information on the item you have chosen. Simply click on the number you wish to change, and enter the new number.

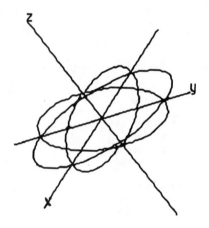

```
Done after 6 iterations

Eigenvalues:

    1.8074        1.0000        7.1926

Eigenvectors:
```

$$\begin{pmatrix} 0.8824 \\ 0.2105 \\ -0.4209 \end{pmatrix} \begin{pmatrix} 0.8824 \\ 0.2105 \\ -0.4209 \end{pmatrix} \begin{pmatrix} 0.8824 \\ 0.2105 \\ -0.4209 \end{pmatrix}$$

```
Original matrix:
```

$$\begin{pmatrix} 3.0000 & -1.0000 & 2.0000 \\ -1.0000 & 2.0000 & -2.0000 \\ 2.0000 & -2.0000 & 5.0000 \end{pmatrix}$$

Sample printout from JACOBIDRAW.

Some Examples to Explore

Try JACOBIDRAW **on the following:**

1. Try JACOBIDRAW on the following matrices, which will give you a sample of all the possibilities:

$$\begin{pmatrix} 2 & -1 & 0 \\ -1 & 2 & -1 \\ 0 & -1 & 2 \end{pmatrix}, \qquad \begin{pmatrix} 2 & -1 & 0 \\ -1 & 2 & -1 \\ 0 & -1 & -2 \end{pmatrix},$$

$$\begin{pmatrix} 2 & -1 & 0 \\ -1 & -2 & -1 \\ 0 & -1 & -2 \end{pmatrix}, \qquad \begin{pmatrix} 0 & -1 & 0 \\ -1 & 0 & -1 \\ 0 & -1 & 0 \end{pmatrix}.$$

16

Fourier

This program graphs the approximation of a given $f(x)$ using Fourier polynomials of different orders. That is, it calculates

$$f(x) = \sum_{n=0}^{k} a_n \cos(nx) + b_n \sin(nx)$$

for a Fourier polynomial of order k.

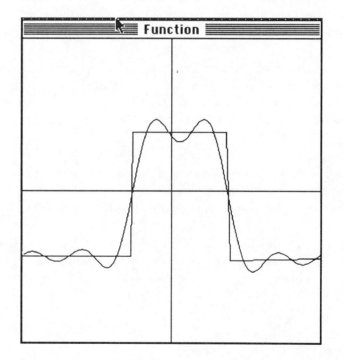

Sample graph from the Fourier *program. This is a third order approximation to the square wave shown.*

The mathematics of Fourier series, and their usefulness in solving boundary value problems in partial differential equations are discussed in detail in Hubbard and West, *Differential Equations: A Dynamical Systems Approach*, Volume III, Chapter 14.

How It Works

On the [Enter] menu, you may choose to enter the function as usual with the keyboard, or graphically as a piecewise linear function by the mouse.

If you choose to enter the function graphically, you may click the mouse anywhere in the main window, which shows the basic period of the function. At the first click the program will only read the y-coordinate and take the left end of the window for the x-coordinate of the first point. You should click again to the right of the first point and a line segment will connect the first point to the second. Continue the process, moving to the right, until the desired function is entered completely, i.e., it should be a piecewise linear function extending all the way to the right end of the window. If you stop before you come to the right end ot the window, the last of the graph piece will be horizontal by default. To assist you in the drawing of the graph you can read off the coordinates of the cursor in the point window.

If you choose to enter the function by formula, a dialog box allows you to enter the expression for the function. Once this is completed, you are asked to enter the period, T, which defaults to 2π. The basic period of the function is the interval from $\pi/2$ for $\pi/2$, which is symmetric about the origin.

Once the graph of the function is on the screen, pull down the [Tasks] menu and choose [Plot Series]. You will be asked if this function has specific symmetries, to speed up the program. You will then see the function approximated, and the order of the Fourier polynomial used registered in the [Order] window.

To stop the approximation you may click the mouse anywhere in the window. It will not stop, however, until the next order appears in the window, which may take up to 30 seconds.

Features

If you know whether the function you entered is even or odd, the time for computation may be reduced by selecting the appropriate item in the dialog box that comes up when you request [Plot Series] from the [Tasks] menu.

If you have entered your function by formula, you are allowed to blow up the graph window to study details of the convergence of the Fourier series.

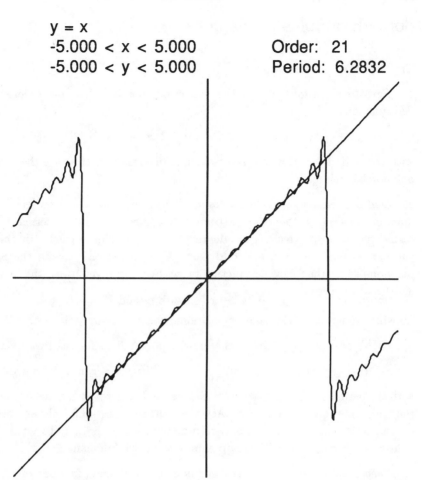

y = x
-5.000 < x < 5.000   Order: 21
-5.000 < y < 5.000   Period: 6.2832

Sample FOURIER *printout.*

Some Examples to Explore

Try FOURIER on the following:

1. *Periodic extensions.* Graph the Fourier polynomials of various orders for the *odd* functions

$$\text{(a)} \quad y = x\,, \qquad \text{(b)} \quad y = 2\arctan(\tan(x/2))$$

with the period 2π. How are the two functions related? How are their Fourier polynomials related?

2. *Odd and even parts of a function.* If you click on $\boxed{\text{Even}}$ or $\boxed{\text{Odd}}$ in the function dialog box, then the program only computes the even terms, i.e., the cosine terms (respectively, the odd terms, i.e., the sine terms). In this way you can extract the even and odd parts of the function. Graph the Fourier polynomials for the following function twice, by clicking on $\boxed{\text{Even}}$ the first time, and $\boxed{\text{Odd}}$ the second.
$$y = 0.2\,x^2 - x \qquad \text{with period 10}\,.$$
To which function do the Fourier polynomials converge in each case?

3. *Gibb's phenomenon.* Graph the Fourier polynomials for the two functions

$$\text{(a)} \quad y = \text{abs}\,(x) \quad (even)\,, \qquad\qquad \text{(b)} \quad y = \text{sgn}\,(x) \quad (odd)$$

with the period 2π. Use $\boxed{\text{Blow up}}$ to see how the Fourier polynomials behave near the endpoints of the period $\pm\pi$. Are the Fourier series uniformly or pointwise convergent in the interior of the period domain $-\pi \le x \le \pi$? To what do the Fourier series converge at the endpoints of the period domain $\pm\pi$?

4. *Subperiods.* Graph the Fourier polynomials for the odd function of period 2:

$$y = \text{sgn}\,(\sin(4\pi x)) \qquad -1 < x < 1 \quad -2 < y < 2\,.$$

Note that the function actually has an even smaller period than 2. How does that show up in the Fourier series?

5. *Out in the wilderness.* Graph the Fourier polynomials for the odd function of period 2:
$$y = \text{sgn}\,(\sin(\pi/x)) \qquad -1 < x < 1 \quad -2 < y < 2\,.$$
Try to blow up around the origin. What happens with the function at the origin? Why do you think the program cannot handle this function properly?

6. *Square pulses.* Graph the Fourier polynomials for the even and odd square pulses by entering them graphically using the cursor.

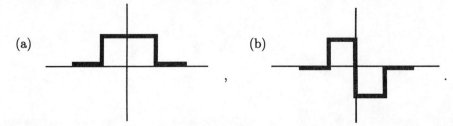

(a)   (b)

17

Planets

This program models the motions of up to ten bodies as they are acted upon by the gravitational or electromagnetic forces between them. The user has the option of specifying the number of planets, the mass, position, and velocity of each of the planets, as well as certain physical characteristics of the universe that these planets inhabit.

You will quickly find how difficult it is to create a system of planets stable enough to stay on the screen. We have included on your disk a number of different possibilities, so that you will have plenty to play with. Playing is the most important thing to do with this program!

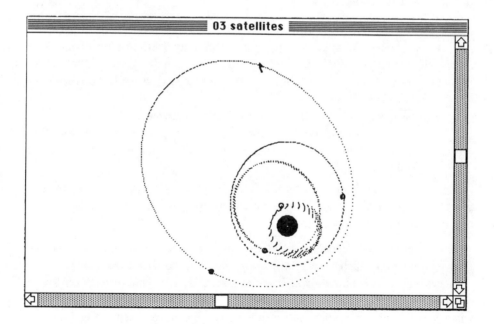

A screen from saved file 03, showing four "planets" and their orbits about a "sun".

To see the simplest interaction between planets, just run the default example. That is, simply choose $\boxed{\text{Start from Current State}}$ or $\boxed{\text{Continue}}$ from the $\boxed{\text{Tasks}}$ menus after starting up the program. Though this example grows old rather quickly, there are many interesting things that you can change to liven up the action.

How It Works

Using the Planet Information Window

You can see and change the specifications of any body. To do so, choose the $\boxed{\text{Show Information Window}}$ from the $\boxed{\text{Tasks}}$ menu, or double click on the body. Next click in the new Information window to make it active, then edit the values in the window.

You will notice that as you change the mass of the body, it grows or shrinks accordingly. Similarly, as you change the position, the body moves. To be able to see graphically what is happening when you change the velocity, you must first select the $\boxed{\text{Velocity}}$ check box. A velocity vector originating at the center of the body will be displayed.

The other check boxes alter other attributes of the body:

- $\boxed{\text{Number}}$ will display the number of the body, in the center of the body if it is large enough, to the lower right if it is not;
- $\boxed{\text{Path}}$, when checked, will cause the body's trajectory to be traced out behind it as it moves;
- $\boxed{\text{Freeze}}$ will "freeze" the body's velocity; a frozen body will move in a straight line, unaffected by other bodies, though it *will* affect all other "unfrozen" bodies. Note that a frozen planet with a velocity of zero will remain stationary.

If you set a planet's mass to zero, it is in some sense the opposite of a "frozen" planet, in that all the other planets with nonzero mass will affect it, but it will not affect any other planets.

A word of caution: because of the way the bodies are drawn on the screen — that is, the parts which overlap are drawn in white so that the edges are clear — occasionally, two planets which are the same size will be exactly on top of one another and they will seem to disappear. This almost never happens except when you are adding bodies; to prevent it, simply move a new body from the default position before adding another one.

To Adjust Position and Velocity with the Mouse

You can also adjust a body's position and velocity graphically with the mouse when you do not need the accuracy of exact numbers. Simply click on the body you wish to alter. The selected body will change from a black circle to a white circle with a black border.

To change its position, click on it and drag it around as you would move an icon around the desktop. To change its velocity, simply click anywhere in the window *except* on the body, and a velocity vector will be displayed, terminating at your cursor. Then drag the tip of the vector around until it is where you want it to be.

If you have a body roughly where you want it, but still need to make minor adjustments, you can double click on the body to bring up its Info window.

To Add and Remove a Body

To add a body, choose Add Body . It will appear at the center of the graph and you can move it to where you want it. You can adjust its specifications graphically or in its Info window.

To remove a body, simply select it by clicking on it (it will turn white, as described before) and then selecting Remove Body from the Change menu.

To Change Settings

Yet another way of adjusting some of the properties of the bodies is with the Settings menu. You can use these menu items to show or hide the numbers, trajectories, or velocity vectors of all the planets at once.

The Trajectories as Lines menu item, when selected, will cause those planetary trajectories that are being shown to be drawn as line segments connecting the dots, rather than as sequences of dots alone.

Tasks

Now a few words about the Tasks menu. A *state* is a set of values for the masses, velocities, and positions of the planets. Two states are defined in the program: the initial state and the current state. What is displayed is always the current state, but the initial state is stored in case you want to return to the initial conditions. (To return to the initial state, select Reset Bodies from the Change menu.) To get the bodies moving, you can select either Start from Current State or Continue . The difference between the two is that in the first case the initial state is set to be the current state, then the simulation begins; whereas in the second case the initial state is unchanged. Note that the Change menu and most of the File menu items are disabled while the simulation is running. To stop the simulation, select Pause .

When the simulation is running, one or more of the planets may move off the screen. If you want to follow them, you can do so by using the scroll bars much like you do for windows on the desktop, except things on the desktop generally don't try to run away from you – so this takes a little practice. Once you have scrolled away from the origin (which is roughly the center of the window you started in) you might have a difficult time scrolling back to it. Instead, simply choose $\boxed{\text{Recenter Planets}}$ from the $\boxed{\text{Tasks}}$ menu. This puts the origin of the planets' plane back in the center of your window. Similarly, if you have changed the size of the Planets window, you can return to the default window size by choosing $\boxed{\text{Default Window Size}}$ from the $\boxed{\text{Tasks}}$ menu.

Features

We have one item left in the $\boxed{\text{Change}}$ menu to discuss: $\boxed{\text{Parameters} \ldots}$. This is the menu item used to alter some of the physical constants of the universe your planets inhabit. The dialog box that comes up offers many choices: first there are the $\boxed{\text{Universe}}$ parameters: $\boxed{\text{Stepsize}}$, $\boxed{\text{Gravity}}$, $\boxed{\text{Friction}}$. Increasing the stepsize will increase the speed at which the simulation runs, but will decrease the accuracy of the model. Conversely, decreasing the stepsize will increase the accuracy, especially of more complicated systems, but will also proportionally slow the calculations.

Universe Parameters   **Universe Bounds**

Step Size: `1.00000`   ● Unbounded
                                ○ Wrap Around Bounds
Friction: `0.00000`   ○ Bounce Off Walls

Force Constant: `1.00000` $\boxed{\text{OK}}$

● Gravity ○ Electrostatics $\boxed{\text{Cancel}}$

Dialog box.

The number you enter as the $\boxed{\text{Force Constant}}$ is a constant which is used to scale the forces the planets exert on each other. $\boxed{\text{Friction}}$ must be a number between zero and one, representing a constant "coefficient of drag" and is used to scale the velocity of the planets.

You can also choose between the force *types* of $\boxed{\text{Gravity}}$ and $\boxed{\text{Electrostatics}}$. With $\boxed{\text{Gravity}}$, two positive masses attract, two negative masses repel, and one of each will chase each other. (This bizarre behavior is actually what classical Newtonian mechanics predicts for "negative" masses.) With $\boxed{\text{Electrostatics}}$, the results are a little more familiar: two like charges repel, two opposite charges attract.

Finally, you can choose the ⎡Universe⎤ bounds to be ⎡Unbounded⎤ (the standard Cartesian plane), or you can ⎡Wrap Around Bounds⎤ (a model of a torus, with which most video game players will be familiar: when a planet goes offscreen at one edge, it comes back at the opposite edge), or you can choose for your bodies to ⎡Bounce Off Walls⎤ (like on a billiard table).

To Print

As in other programs, use the ⎡Print Planets Window⎤ command, or if you do not have a printer handy, you can ⎡Print to File⎤ and later print your files with the ⎡File Printer⎤ program.

Sometimes, if your planetary system has many bodies or if your window is particularly large, not all of the information in a printout will fit on a single page. As a result, when you print to file, it is sometimes necessary to print two pages, each to its own file. The default names for these files are the same except for their suffixes: they will be called "name.p1" and "name.p2". A printout that only requires a single page will be entitled "name.print" to remind you that there was no second page.

As with most things, the best way to learn about PLANETS is by doing, so stop reading and start using the program . . . . Not only is it a mathematical/physical tool for modelling systems too complicated to solve explicitly, it can also be a lot of fun.

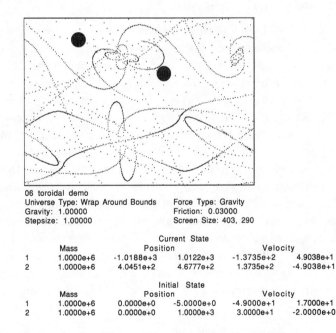

```
06 toroidal demo
Universe Type: Wrap Around Bounds    Force Type: Gravity
Gravity: 1.00000                     Friction: 0.03000
Stepsize: 1.00000                    Screen Size: 403, 290
```

Current State

	Mass	Position		Velocity	
1	1.0000e+6	-1.0188e+3	1.0122e+3	-1.3735e+2	4.9038e+1
2	1.0000e+6	4.0451e+2	4.6777e+2	1.3735e+2	-4.9038e+1

Initial State

	Mass	Position		Velocity	
1	1.0000e+6	0.0000e+0	-5.0000e+0	-4.9000e+1	1.7000e+1
2	1.0000e+6	0.0000e+0	1.0000e+3	3.0000e+1	-2.0000e+0

Sample printout from PLANETS.

Some Examples to Explore

Try PLANETS on the following:

Numbers and names refer to the PLANETS film saved on the **MacMath** disk, courtesy of Trey Jones. Key words in parentheses after the names denote which aspects of the program the examples use or highlight.

1. *Kepler; Kepler.slow.accurate: (gravity; stepsize).* The only difference in these files is the stepsize used in the calculations. In *Kepler*, the stepsize is the default value of 1.0. In *Kepler.slow.accurate*, the stepsize is significantly smaller, 0.05. In *Kepler*, the orbiting planet has a wobble that cannot go undetected after its third or fourth revolution about the larger planet. However, in the second file, *Kepler.slow.accurate*, the smaller planet shows no discernable deviation from its path, even after six or so revolutions. (The smaller stepsize makes this equivalent to 120 revolutions by *Kepler*, timewise — that is, waitwise — so even though six revolutions does not provide reams of data, the point should be quite clear.)

Another small note: the larger planet is not "nailed down". The smaller planet simply does not attract it sufficiently to move it any detectable amount.

2. *Nonharmonic: (gravity; stepsize).* This example reveals some of the limits of this computer model, but is nevertheless useful for teaching a necessary amount of distrust of computers and computer programs, even ones that have been reliable in previous instances.

In this example, two bodies of equal mass start at rest a given distance apart. According to the principle of conservation of momentum and energy, they should oscillate about their center of mass with amplitude equal to their initial separation, if they are not acted on by outside forces. The force that acts on them shows computer error from two sources; incomplete modelling of reality and roundoff error. As the distance separating the two bodies approaches zero, the attractive force approaches infinity. In our model, planets can pass through each other, getting arbitrarily close to one another, up to the accuracy of the computer. Thus they can approach as if they were point masses, up to the point where they would have to be subatomic particles to get that close in the physical world, in which case gravity would be the least of the forces upon them. In real life, of course, two planets would slam right into each other, and that would be that. So, our planets can pass very close, and then fling themselves off into space with rather extreme velocities, corresponding to a dramatic gain in mechanical energy. (This is similar to the effect of numerical tunneling in the double well potential problem — experiment #5 in Section 13, **2D Iterations**.) More on that in a moment ... .

Another problem is that roundoff error means that we must approximate the gravity well of a body with a piecewise linear approximation (which rounds to zero at larger distances). After the planets have attained a sufficient separation, they are free of each other, and have reached a sort of "terminal velocity". Thus the planets can start off having only a negative potential energy and end up having only a positive kinetic energy. The distance separating the planets just before they pass and fling each other off into never-never land varies with the stepsize. This distance in turn affects the terminal velocities. Since stepsize is defined, and terminal velocity readily available, some sample data are presented in the following table:

Stepsize	Terminal velocity
1.0	-238.1
0.9	336.8
0.8	74.8
0.7	93.0
0.6	115.6
0.5	$-3\,054.0$
0.4	192.0
0.3	279.6
0.2	615.0
0.1	-400.7

The negative values in the table indicate that the planets barely passed each other, then, due to extreme gravitational forces, performed an about-face, and flew off the way they had come, and right into the face of all of Physics. Such are the consequences of discrete modelling of continuous processes. (Thanks to Tony Yan for pointing out that most PLANETS-type computer models fail to conserve energy.)

3. *Binary – 5 planets; pairs; retro pairs; satellites; (gravity).* These four files are mostly just neat to look at, and they show how PLANETS can be used to model quite interesting systems. A note on these systems: The main reason most are binary systems of some type is that it is often easier to "design" binary systems if you want to avoid having to "nail down" one or more of your planets. In my experience, it is often difficult to get the net momentum of a system to zero when there is a central body, and orbiting bodies with any significant proportion of its mass. It's easier just to make the masses more nearly equal, and let them both spin.

Planet number 5 in *Binary – 5 planets* is actually unstable, and gets flung off into deep space after a few minutes (but don't bother to wait unless you are running on a Mac II, it's not *that* exciting), even though it doesn't seem unstable at the beginning. (Planet 5 is the outer one of the subsystem initially on the left.)

The only difference between *pairs* and *retro pairs* is that in *pairs* both binary systems rotate the same way. In *retro pairs* the rotation of one pair is retrograde with respect to the other.

Notice that the *satellites* are all massless, so it is quite trivial to set up such a system.

4. *Binary and orbit: (gravity).* This is another interesting file. As you watch the small planet orbit around the two central stars, it seems to become unstable, but after quite a bit of run time, it defines a not-too-wide band that it likes to stay in (if you have the path showing — and that's the default setting). Note that the gravitational force between the two central stars varies periodically.

5. *Interesting thing: (gravity).* This one mostly shows off the numbering, which is outside the actual planet because it is so small. It is also rather interesting because, in order to get such small bodies to attract, gravity has been hyped up to 500 times normal. Just watching is interesting, too, because at first it is unclear what the bodies are doing, or whether there is any rhyme or reason here. But watch for a bit, and it becomes clear.

6. *Toroidal demo: (gravity; torus).* This system gives a quick introduction to the bizzare physics on the torus model, i.e., Wrap Around Bounds . Referring to a marked printout beforehand is perhaps the easiest way to see what's going on. There is a position where the gravity will suddenly reverse its x or y coordinate direction. This is when the shortest path between two bodies suddenly jumps from crossing an "edge" to not crossing one (there aren't any edges on the torus, only on the representation used to map it onto the computer screen).

7. *Mag-neat-o-bizzar-o; toroidal spirals; (electrostatics/gravity with friction; torus).* The names say it all. We have two bodies of equal mass (or charge), and we are modelling their behavior on a torus as they are acted on by their mutual electrostatic repulsion. Note a few things: First, the motion of the planets is symmetric about two vertical lines as well as two horizontal lines, and the places where these lines cross on the surface of the torus define four lattice points (it may look like six, but the ones on the edges are the same), and each of these four points is a sort of basin of repulsion. These are the places that the charged bodies like to avoid each other. Compare this to the similar, but opposite, pattern in the file *toroidal spirals*. Next, note that the charges seem to defy the laws of physics because they keep a relatively constant pace — on an unbounded plane, the repulsion between the two bodies would continue to accelerate them until they became far enough separated that they had no more effect on each other. Actually, though, each of the four "lattice points" is in some sense equivalent to the origin, or they take turns being the origin as the bodies move from place to place. Since the motion of the planets is always symmetric with respect to

one of these points, their net momentum is always zero if we choose the right origin. A similar situation occurs in *toroidal spirals*. In the file *toroidal spirals*, we again get four lattice points, and these are four basins of attraction. A 2% frictional force has been added to counteract the strange way the planets on the torus defy physicists' rules: in an unbounded plane, two planets flying past each other will continually slow down; but here they continually speed up — as they fly away from each other, they only get closer because of the wrap-around effect.

8.   *Electro-billiards orbit:* (*electrostatics; bouncing off walls*). In this rather bizarre system, we have two electrically charged bodies, one of which is nailed down in the center of the screen. The world is a billiards table (Bounce off Walls), and the second body moves in a sort of anti-orbit around the first, repulsed by both it and the walls.

9.   *Billiards:* (*gravity; bouncing off walls*). The main purpose of this system is to explain why there aren't more like it — they aren't too terribly exciting, because the bouncing off the walls tends to mess up the symmetry of the system unless its center is at the center of the window. Even then, the graceful curves of the bodies are disrupted, though this one does trace a fairly nice design. Some friction has been added to counteract the gain of energy (due to discretization) during close encounters.

10.   *Harmonics; harmonics in 2D:* (*electrostatics; torus*). In the first system, *harmonics*, two electrically charged bodies on a torus start with a slight velocity straight away from each other. Since the bodies repel each other in the opposite direction as they move toward the "edge", they begin to oscillate. In fact, their motion is simple harmonic motion (SHM), and can be described in terms of $\sin(nt)$ for some n.

   In the second system, we have a symmetric pair of symmetric pairs; and as the four bodies move, they undergo SHM in two dimensions. For the reader who is experienced with parametric equations, the shapes traced out by the bodies should be familiar. They are *Lissajous* figures, defined parametrically by

$$(x, y) \quad = \quad \Big(\sin(nt) \, , \, \cos(mt) \Big)$$

for some m and n. The constants m and n are determined by the spacing of the bodies at the beginning.

11.   *Pseudo harmonics; pseudo harmonics in 2D:* (*electrostatics; torus*). In these examples, we have bodies that oscillate, but not harmonically. We start, in the first file, with four bodies aligned in a straight line on a torus. Because of their uneven spacing, the motion of the bodies is not regular.

   In the second file, this effect of irregular motion is even more pronounced, and only the extremely symmetrical placement of the bodies keeps everything from flying apart.

12.   *Negative mass; negative mass 1%; negative mass 5%: (gravity (sort of); torus).* These systems are clearly nothing but an exercise in theoretical physics, but they are nonetheless very interesting. In the first, *negative mass*, we start with two planets of equal but opposite mass. The negative mass is not anti-matter; anti-matter particles have the opposite spin and charge, but the same mass, of their normal counterparts. Instead, *negative mass*, and the behavior of these systems, is a product of pathological applications of standard physical equations.

Suppose we have a mass m and an equal negative mass $-m$. Then the gravitational force between them is defined as

$$F \;=\; G \frac{(m)\,(-m)}{r \times r}$$

in the direction along the line from one body to the other, where G is a constant and r is the distance between them. Note that F is negative, since one of the masses is negative. According to the basic formula $F = ma$, the acceleration on the positive mass will be negative, that is, in the direction away from the other mass. However, the negative mass has a positive acceleration (in the usual direction), and so takes off in pursuit of the first mass. Since the masses have similar magnitudes, so do their accelerations, and they maintain a constant separation as they continue to accelerate. Still, this does not violate any of the laws of physics, because the net mass of the system is zero; the net kinetic energy and momentum are also both zero.

As the system evolves, a strange thing happens. Becauses these masses live on a torus, as they move, their velocities become such that their displacement with each step in time is close to the height of the screen (one of the circumferences of the torus), and they appear to move very little, and change directions in weird ways. When the displacement reaches twice the screen height, the planets disappear and never come back. This seems to be an artifact of the program, since on a torus it should not be possible to disappear.

The other two files have 1% and 5% frictional forces added, giving the planets terminal velocities. Also, all of these systems are not quite aligned vertically, so that they move to the right; this makes their behavior more easily observable.

18

Linear Dynamical Systems

Linear dynamical systems (whether they be linear differential equations with constant coefficients or iterative systems) are the only important class of higher dimensional systems that can be solved in terms of elementary functions.

They can be written in vector and matrix notation as

$$\mathbf{x}' = A\mathbf{x} \qquad \text{or} \qquad \mathbf{x}_{n+1} = A\mathbf{x}_n , \tag{1}$$

respectively, for differential or iterative systems.

In the case of two dependent variables, these systems can be written

$$\begin{pmatrix} x \\ y \end{pmatrix}' = \begin{pmatrix} a & b \\ c & d \end{pmatrix} \begin{pmatrix} x \\ y \end{pmatrix} , \qquad \begin{pmatrix} x_{n+1} \\ y_{n+1} \end{pmatrix} = \begin{pmatrix} a & b \\ c & d \end{pmatrix} \begin{pmatrix} x_n \\ y_n \end{pmatrix} \tag{2}$$

or more explicitly as

$$\frac{dx}{dt} = ax + by , \qquad x_{n+1} = ax_n + by_n ,$$
$$\frac{dy}{dt} = cx + dy , \qquad y_{n+1} = cx_n + dy_n . \tag{3}$$

The solutions to these linear dynamical systems can usually be written, respectively, as

$$\mathbf{x} = C_1 e^{\lambda_1 t} + C_2 e^{\lambda_2 t} , \qquad \mathbf{x} = C_1 \lambda_1{}^n + C_2 \lambda_2{}^n , \tag{4}$$

where λ_1 and λ_2 are the eigenvalues of the matrix. We shall review how to find eigenvalues, after a few comments about how the form of equations (4) give important information about behaviors of trajectories or orbits in the xy-plane.

The behaviors of the solutions $\mathbf{x}$ to a linear dynamical system with respect to an equilibrium or fixed point are classified first as *sinks* (contraction); *sources* (expansion); or *saddles* (contraction in one direction, expansion in another). They are also classified by whether or not they *spiral*, and, in the case of iteration, as to whether they involve *flips*, as discussed back in Example 3.4 and further illustrated below. The behaviors resulting from the positions of λ_1 and λ_2 in equations (4) are:

for differential equations:

Sinks: Re $\lambda_1 < 0$;   Re $\lambda_2 < 0$.
Saddles: Re $\lambda_1 < 0$;   Re $\lambda_2 > 0$.
Sources: Re $\lambda_1 > 0$;   Re $\lambda_2 > 0$.

Spirals occur when λ_1 and λ_2 are complex conjugates of each other.

for iteration:

Sinks: $|\lambda_1| < 1$; $|\lambda_2| < 1$.
Saddles: $|\lambda_1| < 1$; $|\lambda_2| > 1$.
Sources: $|\lambda_1| > 1$; $|\lambda_2| > 1$.

Spirals occur when λ_1 and λ_2 are complex conjugates of each other.

No flips: $\lambda_1 > 0$; $\lambda_2 > 0$.
Single flip: $\lambda_1 < 0$; $\lambda_2 > 0$.
Double flip: $\lambda_1 < 0$; $\lambda_2 < 0$.

The behaviors for differential equations were well illustrated in Section 2, but those for iteration are less obvious in static pictures. We can alleviate that problem by connecting successive points of an iteration orbit by line segments. We show this here in detail for a single orbit of a sink; the other possibilities are shown (for four orbits each) in the summary iteration diagram below.

Example 18.1.   In each of the following examples, the orbit always begins at P_0 in the upper left-hand corner. The picture on the left then shows a single orbit as dots only; the picture on the right shows the dots connected in order.

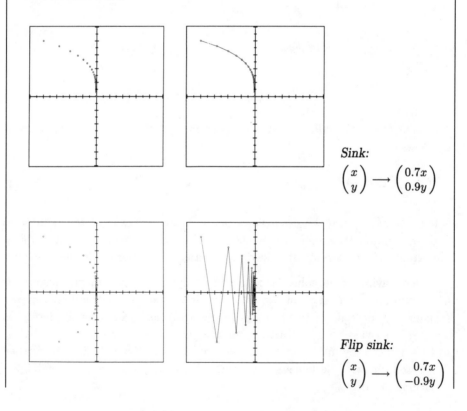

Sink:
$$\begin{pmatrix} x \\ y \end{pmatrix} \longrightarrow \begin{pmatrix} 0.7x \\ 0.9y \end{pmatrix}$$

Flip sink:
$$\begin{pmatrix} x \\ y \end{pmatrix} \longrightarrow \begin{pmatrix} 0.7x \\ -0.9y \end{pmatrix}$$

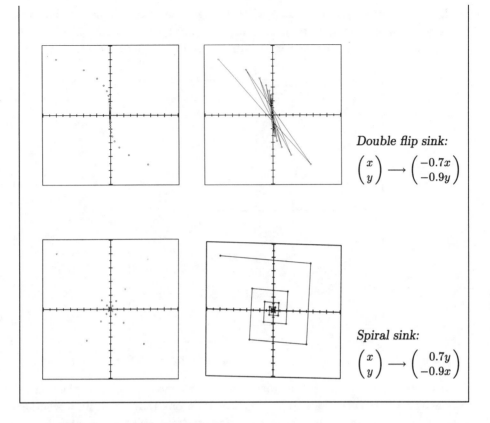

Double flip sink:
$$\begin{pmatrix} x \\ y \end{pmatrix} \longrightarrow \begin{pmatrix} -0.7x \\ -0.9y \end{pmatrix}$$

Spiral sink:
$$\begin{pmatrix} x \\ y \end{pmatrix} \longrightarrow \begin{pmatrix} 0.7y \\ -0.9x \end{pmatrix}$$

The relationship of the values of λ_1 and λ_2 to the original matrix A is best understood in terms of eigenvalues and eigenvectors.

Recall that a number λ is an *eigenvalue* of a matrix A if there exists a nonzero vector $\mathbf{v}$ such that $A\mathbf{v} = \lambda\mathbf{v}$. Then $\mathbf{v}$ is called a corresponding *eigenvector*. Recall also that the *trace* of a matrix is the sum of the main diagonal terms: $\operatorname{tr} A = a + d$, and that the *determinant* of a 2×2 matrix is $\det A = ad - bc$.

The eigenvalues are the solutions of the equation $\lambda^2 - (\operatorname{tr} A)\lambda + \det A = 0$, so

$$\lambda = \frac{\operatorname{tr} A \pm \sqrt{(\operatorname{tr} A)^2 - 4\det A}}{2} \tag{5}$$

Since from equation (5) we see that the eigenvalues are determined by the trace and the determinant, behaviors can be classified by the position of a matrix A in the trace-determinant plane. Thus for any linear dynamical system you can calculate $\operatorname{tr} A$ and $\det A$, then know immediately from the following diagrams what the xy-plane behavior will look like. But, as you can see from the table preceding Example 18.1, the division of the trace-determinant plane in the two cases is different for *expansion/contraction behaviors*, because of the different position of the eigenvalues in the solutions (4).

In a differential equation, the *signs* of the eigenvalues determine whether trajectories expand (from a *source*), contract (to a *sink*), or expand in the direction of one eigenvector and contract in the direction of the other (a *saddle*).

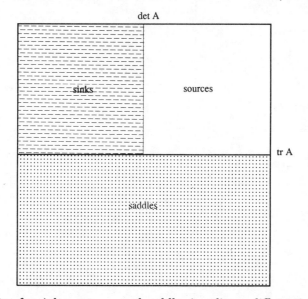

Bifurcation for sinks, sources, and saddles in a linear differential equation.

In an iterative system, on the other hand, it is the *absolute values* of the eigenvalues and whether they are greater or less than one that determines whether the mapping expands (from a *source*), contracts (to a *sink*), or expands in the direction of one eigenvector and contracts in the direction of the other (a *saddle*).

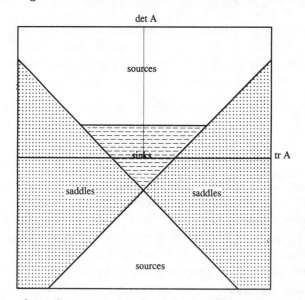

Bifurcation for sinks, sources, and saddles in a linear iterative equation.

For both differential equations and iteration, equation (5) shows that the parabola $(\operatorname{tr} A)^2 = 4 \det A$ separates *spiral behaviors* (due to imaginary parts of the λ's) from nonspiral behaviors.

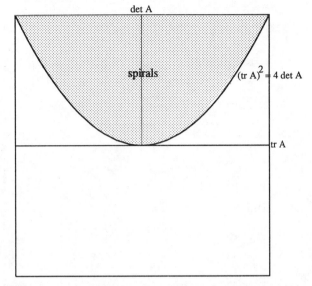

Bifurcation for spirals in any linear dynamical system.

Furthermore, in an iterative system, the *signs* of the eigenvalues determine an additional behavior not found in differential equations: a negative eigenvalue introduces a *flip*, and two negative eigenvalues introduce a *double flip* (illustrated in Example 18.1).

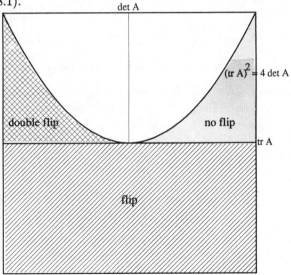

Bifurcation for flips in a linear iterative equation.

Comprehensive *summary* bifurcation diagrams for differential equations and for iteration are given on the next two pages.

Summary Bifurcation Diagram for Two-dimensional Differential Equations

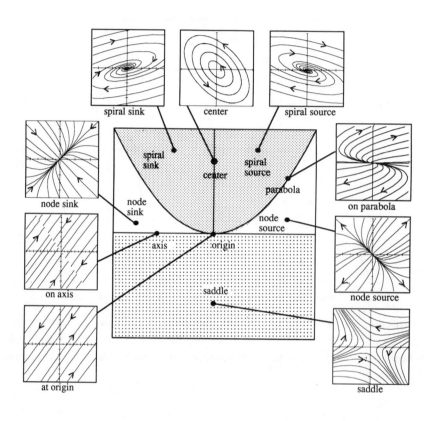

For a linear differential equation.

The pictures surrounding the bifurcation diagrams show typical xy-plane
1 behaviors in each of the different regions. Those for iteration, on the opposite
page, show exactly *four* orbits in each case.

For sources, the four orbits begin close to the origin, one in each quadrant.		*For sinks, the four orbits begin on the outside corners, one in each quadrant.*	
For saddles, the four orbits begin at outside points, near the horizontal axis, one in each quadrant.		*For centers, the four orbits begin on the first quadrant diagonal.*	

The points of each orbit are connected in order, P_0 to P_1 to $P_2 \ldots$. An arrow
is placed in the first line segment of the orbits, from P_0 to P_1.

Summary Bifurcation Diagram for Two-dimensional Iterative Dynamical Systems

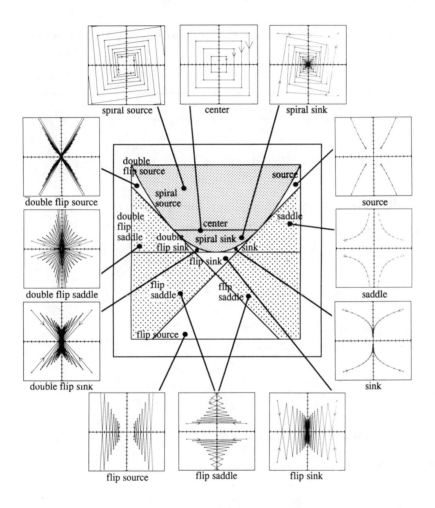

For a linear iterative system.

Linearization

Whenever you have a nonlinear system, it can be approximated by a *linearization*, which usually will have the same phase plane behaviors near each singularity. A good example is given in Example 2.5, which we expand here as Example 18.2.

In the case of two dependent variables, the formulas for linearizing a nonlinear system are as follows:

$$\mathbf{L\,I\,N\,E\,A\,R\,I\,Z\,A\,T\,I\,O\,N} \quad \text{about} \quad (x_0, y_0)$$

$$\frac{dx}{dt} = f(x,y) \approx f(x_0, y_0) + \left.\frac{\partial f}{\partial x}\right|_{(x_0,y_0)} (x - x_0) + \left.\frac{\partial f}{\partial y}\right|_{(x_0,y_0)} (y - y_0) \,.$$

$$\frac{dy}{dt} = g(x,y) \approx g(x_0, y_0) + \left.\frac{\partial g}{\partial x}\right|_{(x_0,y_0)} (x - x_0) + \left.\frac{\partial g}{\partial y}\right|_{(x_0,y_0)} (y - y_0) \,.$$

When expanding around a singularity (x_0, y_0), this simplifies to

$$\frac{d(x - x_0)}{dt} \approx \left.\frac{\partial f}{\partial x}\right|_{(x_0,y_0)} (x - x_0) + \left.\frac{\partial f}{\partial y}\right|_{(x_0,y_0)} (y - y_0) \,,$$

$$\frac{d(y - y_0)}{dt} \approx \left.\frac{\partial g}{\partial x}\right|_{(x_0,y_0)} (x - x_0) + \left.\frac{\partial g}{\partial y}\right|_{(x_0,y_0)} (y - y_0) \,,$$

with the linearization matrix

$$A\Big|_{(x_0,y_0)} = \begin{pmatrix} \dfrac{\partial f}{\partial x} & \dfrac{\partial f}{\partial y} \\[2mm] \dfrac{\partial g}{\partial x} & \dfrac{\partial g}{\partial y} \end{pmatrix}\Bigg|_{(x_0,y_0)}$$

Example 18.2.
$$\frac{dx}{dt} = y(x + 1) \,,$$
$$\frac{dy}{dt} = (3 - y)x \,.$$

The linearization matrix in this case is given by

$$A\Big|_{(x_0,y_0)} = \begin{pmatrix} \dfrac{\partial f}{\partial x} & \dfrac{\partial f}{\partial y} \\[2mm] \dfrac{\partial g}{\partial x} & \dfrac{\partial g}{\partial y} \end{pmatrix}\Bigg|_{(x_0,y_0)} = \begin{pmatrix} y_0 & x_0 + 1 \\[2mm] 3 - y_0 & -x_0 \end{pmatrix}$$

There are two singularities, at $(0,0)$ and $(-1, 3)$.

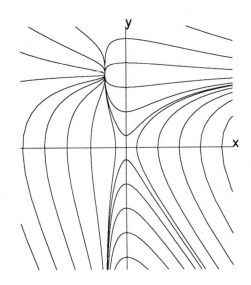

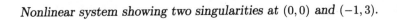

Nonlinear system showing two singularities at $(0,0)$ and $(-1,3)$.

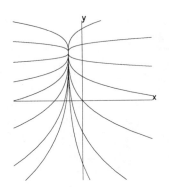

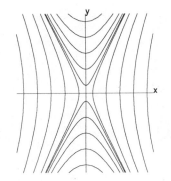

Linearization about $(-1,3)$

$$A\Big|_{(-1,3)} = \begin{pmatrix} 3 & 0 \\ 0 & 1 \end{pmatrix}.$$

SOURCE

Linearization about $(0,0)$

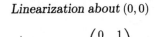

$$A\Big|_{(0,0)} = \begin{pmatrix} 0 & 1 \\ 3 & 0 \end{pmatrix}.$$

SADDLE

19

Bifurcations

You may well wonder what causes the dramatic changes in phase plane behavior discussed in Section 9, DiffEq, Phase Plane, under "Bifurcation". The following discussion deals exclusively with the case of an autonomous differential equation in two variables:

$$\frac{dx}{dt} = f(x,y) , \qquad \frac{dy}{dt} = g(x,y) .$$

Much of the explanation lies in the relative position of the *nullclines*, the curves in the xy-plane that show where slopes are vertical (where $dx/dt = 0$) and horizontal (where $dy/dt = 0$). In the pictures in this section, the nullclines are dotted curves showing where the vertical and horizontal slopes are zero; sample trajectories are solid curves, as usual. Singularities or equillibria occur when both derivatives are simultaneously zero, which mean the points where the nullclines cross.

Example 19.1.

The nullcline information at the right is combined to produce the spiral source below.

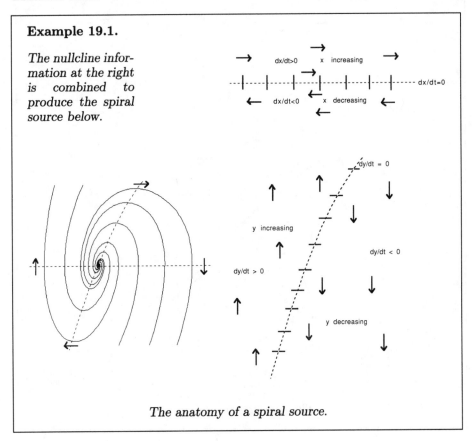

The anatomy of a spiral source.

131

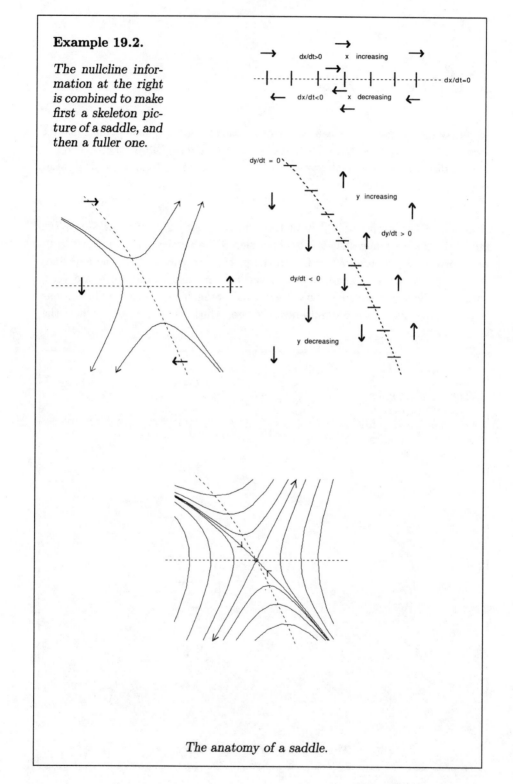

Example 19.2.

*The nullcline infor-
mation at the right
is combined to make
first a skeleton pic-
ture of a saddle, and
then a fuller one.*

dx/dt>0   x increasing

dx/dt=0

dx/dt<0   x decreasing

dy/dt = 0

y increasing

dy/dt > 0

dy/dt < 0

y decreasing

The anatomy of a saddle.

If the differential equation furthermore depends upon two parameters, a and b, then the position of the vertical and horizontal nullclines will depend upon a and b as well. This may produce sudden changes in the nature of the singularities, and thus change the long term (limiting) behavior of solutions to the differential equation. Such a change is called a *bifurcation*. The DIFFEQ, PHASE PLANE program detects two standard types of local bifurcation: the saddle-node bifurcation and the sink-source bifurcation.

The Saddle-Node Bifurcation

Consider the summary bifurcation diagram for linear differential equations given in Section 18,

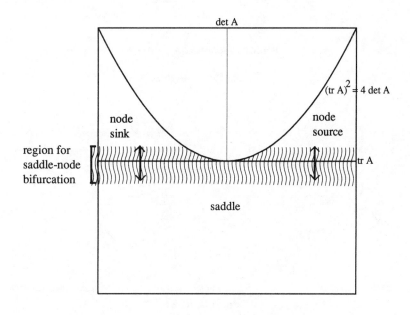

Paths of singularities in trace-determinant diagram when we gently change parameters a and b.

where A is the linearization matrix. What happens when a change in parameters a and b causes $\det A$ to pass through zero? Only rarely can a node turn into a saddle — the far more usual result is that a node and a saddle annihilate each other. In the typical case, saddle-node bifurcation involves the creation or a destruction of a pair of singularities consisting of a saddle and a node.

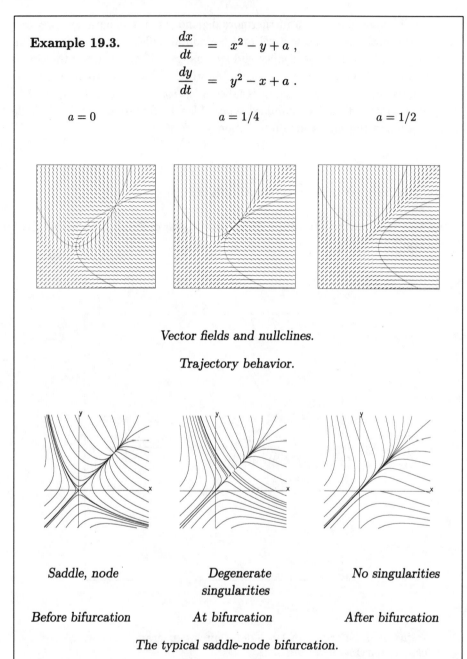

Example 19.3.

$$\frac{dx}{dt} = x^2 - y + a ,$$

$$\frac{dy}{dt} = y^2 - x + a .$$

$a = 0$ $\qquad\qquad\qquad$ $a = 1/4$ $\qquad\qquad\qquad$ $a = 1/2$

Vector fields and nullclines.

Trajectory behavior.

Saddle, node $\qquad$ *Degenerate singularities* $\qquad$ *No singularities*

Before bifurcation $\qquad$ *At bifurcation* $\qquad$ *After bifurcation*

The typical saddle-node bifurcation.

At the bifurcation point ($a = \frac{1}{4}$ in Example 19.3), the vertical and horizontal nullclines meet *tangentially* at a single point. Before the bifurcation they intersect each other at two points; the saddle and the node. After the bifurcation, they no longer intersect each other, i.e., the saddle and node have coalesced and disappeared.

The only exception (and it is a most unusual extreme exception) to this general behavior occurs if the bifurcation actually produces a string of singularities as shown in the figure below. In that case, an isolated saddle is exchanged for an isolated node. In this case, the nullclines coincide for more than a single point. For instance, in the example below, you might think of the nullclines as rotating in opposite directions around the equilibrium point.

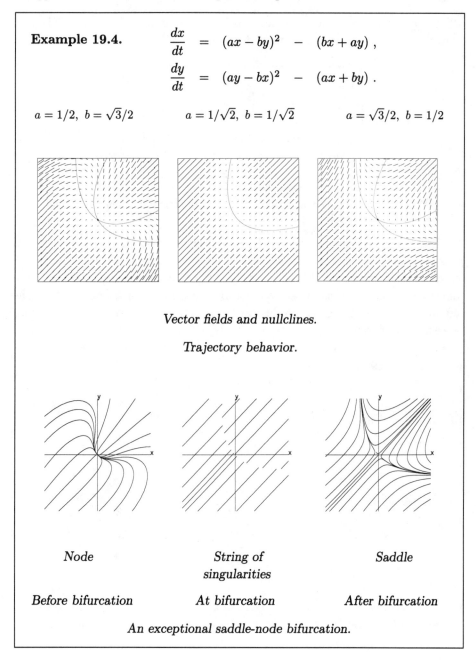

Example 19.4.
$$\frac{dx}{dt} = (ax - by)^2 - (bx + ay),$$
$$\frac{dy}{dt} = (ay - bx)^2 - (ax + by).$$

$a = 1/2, \ b = \sqrt{3}/2$ \qquad $a = 1/\sqrt{2}, \ b = 1/\sqrt{2}$ \qquad $a = \sqrt{3}/2, \ b = 1/2$

Vector fields and nullclines.

Trajectory behavior.

Node \qquad\qquad *String of singularities* \qquad\qquad *Saddle*

Before bifurcation \qquad\qquad *At bifurcation* \qquad\qquad *After bifurcation*

An exceptional saddle-node bifurcation.

The program DIFFEQ, PHASE PLANE only checks where det $A = 0$. Therefore, you yourself must locate singularities before and after the bifurcation to make sure that it really is a *typical* saddle-node bifurcation.

The Sink-Source Bifurcation

To change a sink into a source, we again refer to the summary bifurcation diagram for linear differential equations in Section 18.

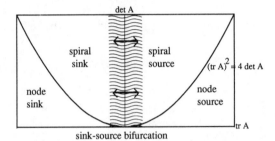

Paths of singularities in trace-determinant diagram when we change parameters a and b.

There we note that sink-source bifurcation requires passing through the region of spiral sinks and sources, so we are, in reality, changing a spiral sink into a spiral source. At the bifurcation point, the linearization has zero trace, so in the linearized case, the center is surrounded by a continuum of nested cycles. The nonlinear terms of the equation destroy these cycles, and turn the "center" into a weak sink or source.

Example 19.5.
Sink-source bifurcation

$$\frac{dx}{dt} = y,$$

$$\frac{dy}{dt} = (a - x^2)y - x.$$

$a = -1/2$ $a = 0$ $a = 1/2$

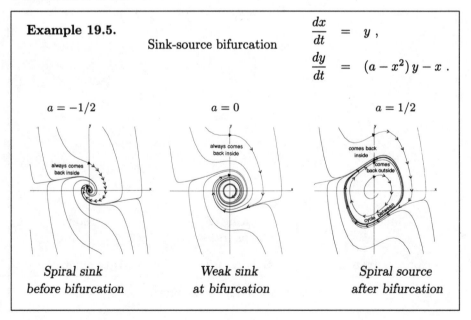

Spiral sink   *Weak sink*   *Spiral source*
before bifurcation   *at bifurcation*   *after bifurcation*

Suppose that we pass from a spiral sink to a weak sink to a spiral source. At the point of bifurcation, a neighboring point (x_*, y_*) can be found, which after one turn has come closer to the singularity. Changing ever so slightly the singularity into a source, the point (x_*, y_*) will still have to come closer after one turn. But points in the immediate neighborhood of the singularity are now forced to spiral outwards! Since the closest points spiral outwards and the farther away points still spiral inwards, somewhere in between there must be a point which after one turn does neither, i.e., it returns to itself. That's a cycle. This typical formation of a limit cycle between a weak spiral of one type and an outer spiral behavior of the opposite type is called a *Hopf bifurcation*.

The only loophole to creation or destruction of a cycle is when the bifurcation point produces a continuum of cycles surrounding the singularity. The program only checks for the trace of the linearization being zero at the bifurcation point. Therefore you yourself must locate singularities before and after the bifurcation to make sure that it really is a typical sink-source bifurcation.

Topological Charge

A physicist will typically ask "is there some conservation law for bifurcation behavior?" The answer is yes — the conserved quantity is called "topological charge", which is explained in terms of "winding number" as follows.

Suppose you surround an isolated singularity with a closed curve γ, in our pictures a circle. At each point on the curve, the vector field $(dx/dt,\ dy/dt)$ will thus specify a direction, which changes as you go around γ. When you return to the same point on γ, the vector must have rotated an integral number on times, the *winding number of the curve*. This integer is called the *topological charge of the singularity*.

Example 19.6.   Calculation of winding number.

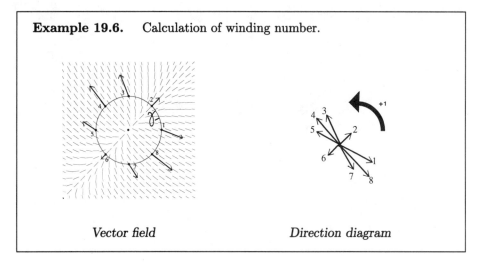

Vector field   Direction diagram

Example 19.7.

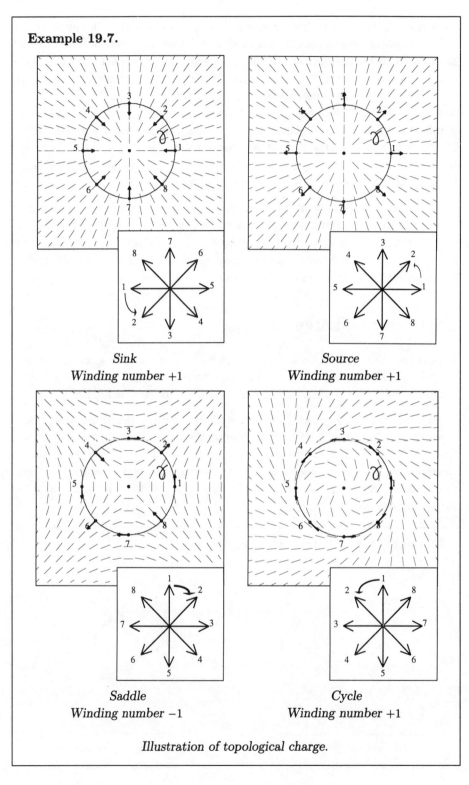

Sink
Winding number +1

Source
Winding number +1

Saddle
Winding number −1

Cycle
Winding number +1

Illustration of topological charge.

Notice that a node has charge $+1$ while a saddle has charge -1 (the sign is the same as the determinant of the linearization at the singularity). The importance of the topological charges is due to the following properties:

(1) *The topological charge is additive*, i.e., if the closed curve surrounds several singularities, then the winding number of *the curve* is the sum of all the topological charges of the singularities enclosed.

(2) *The topological charge is conserved*, i.e., it is invariant under change of parameters as long as the curve is not intersected by a singularity. This is because the winding number must depend continuously on the parameters a and b. Since it is an integer, it therefore cannot change its value. The only loophole is when a singularity hits the curve, thus making the direction, and hence the winding number, undefined.

Since saddles and nodes have opposite charges, we therefore see that, in general, a saddle or a node cannot be created or destroyed singly, only in pairs (cf. the behavior of particles and antiparticles in high energy physics). The only loophole is the bifurcations which create a string of singularities.

20

Numerical Approximation

MacMath applies standard numerical methods to two tasks, integration of a function of a single variable (in ANALYZER), and in the drawing of solutions to differential equations (in all DIFFEQ programs, NUMERICAL METHODS, 1D PERIODIC EQUATIONS, and PLANETS).

Integration

For a function of a single variable, $y = f(t)$, the problem is to calculate the area, $\int_{t_0}^{t_f} f(t)\, dt$, under a curve over a given t-interval.

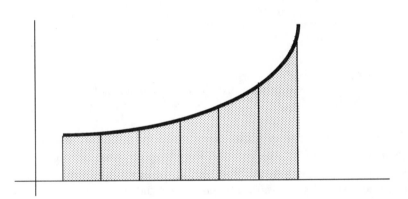

Subdividing area under $y = f(t)$ into $n = 6$ vertical panels.

The function $f(t)$ gives the *height* f_i of the panel used in each subinterval. The independent variable (horizontal axis) interval is divided into n subintervals, each of width $h = (t_f - t_0)/n$, and the idea is to let $n \to \infty$, or $h \to 0$.

For numerical integration, $\int_{t_0}^{t_f} f(t)\, dt$, the idea is to calculate the area under a curve by subdividing it into vertical slices of width h.

$$\text{Area} \quad \approx \quad hf_0 + hf_1 + hf_2 + \cdots + hf_{n-1} \quad = \quad h\sum_{i=0}^{n-1} f_i \,.$$

The only question is where and how to measure f_i to give a reasonable "average" value over the whole subinterval. There are a number of different methods, which we would like to introduce before discussing why they are classified by different "orders".

First Order Methods

For a Riemann left-hand sum, the f_i for each subinterval is the value of the function at its left-hand endpoint; the width of each panel is h.

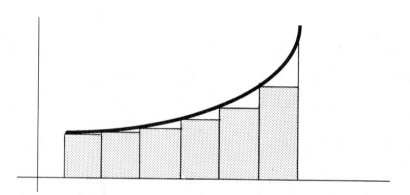

Approximating area by the left-hand method.

To improve the accuracy of this numerical approximation, you use a smaller stepsize. Try sketching it by hand on the above drawing, halving the stepsize. Draw new panels using the same method on the new subintervals. Your approximation of area will better fill the region under the curve.

An alternative first order method would use the right-hand endpoints.

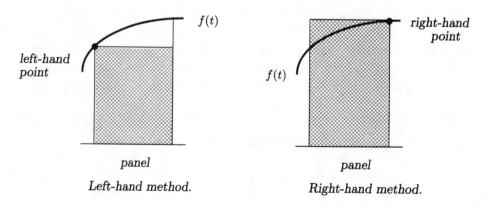

Left-hand method.   *Right-hand method.*

Second Order Methods

The *trapezoidal* and *midpoint* methods approximate the line segment with *sloped lines* (i.e., the panels are being approximated with trapezoids, and the function f is being approximated by a *piecewise linear function*). The trapezoidal method uses the *secant* joining the left-hand point and the right-hand point. The midpoint method uses the *tangent* through the midpoint.

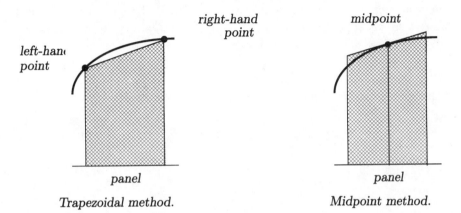

Trapezoidal method.   Midpoint method.

Notes:

The *trapezoidal* method averages left-hand and right-hand methods.

Any line through the *midpoint* will produce the same result. ANALYZER actually draws the horizontal line, which is easier to compute, and which you can use even if the function is not differentiable at the midpoint.

Fourth Order Method

Simpson's method approximates the line segment with the *parabola* going through the left-hand point, the midpoint, and the right-hand point (i.e., the function f is approximated by a *piecewise quadratic function*).

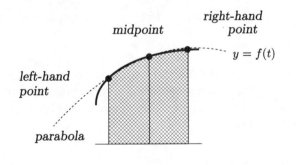

Simpson's method.

Differential Equations

The problem is to draw the solution $x = u(t)$ to $x' = f(t, x)$.

The differential equation $x' = f(t, x)$ gives the *slope* m_i used in each subinterval. The independent variable (horizontal axis) interval is divided into n subintervals, each of width h, and the idea is to let $n \to \infty$, or $h \to 0$.

For a first order differential equation $x' = f(t, x)$, the idea of a numerical method is simply repeated linear approximation, with a *stepsize* h that determines successive t values:

$$t_1 = t_0 + h, \quad t_2 = t_1 + h, \quad \ldots \quad t_{i+1} = t_i + h,$$

and the approximation formula is given in terms of the *slope* m_i:

$$x_1 \approx x_0 + m_0 h, \quad \ldots, \quad x_{i+1} \approx x_i + m_i h = x_0 + h \sum_{i=0}^{n-1} m_i .$$

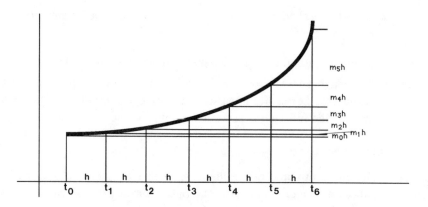

Approximate solution to differential equation, over 6 steps with stepsize h.

The only question is where and how to measure m_i to give a reasonable "average" value over the whole subinterval. There are a number of different methods, which we would like to introduce before discussing why they are classified by different "orders".

First Order Methods

For *Euler's method*, the simplest, you start at a point (t_0, x_0) representing your initial condition, take a step in the direction of the slope $x'(t_0) = f(t_0, x_0)$, and land at (t_1, x_1). There you recalculate the slope $x'(t_1) = f(t_1, x_1)$, take another step, and land at (t_2, x_2). By repeating this process, you (or the computer) define the approximate Euler solution to the differential equation.

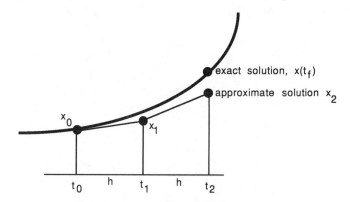

Approximating a solution by Euler's method.

To improve the accuracy of an Euler approximation, you use a smaller stepsize. Try sketching it by hand, on the above drawing, halving the stepsize. Use a slope for each step parallel to the slope of the "exact" solution pictured; your new approximation will end up closer to the right-hand point of the "exact" solution.

For differential equations, we only know the left-hand endpoint; the job is to estimate the right-hand one. Euler approximations will converge upon the actual solution, but rather slowly. Two of the most popular improvements on Euler approximations do a bit of "sniffing ahead" to see how much the slope will change during each step.

Second Order Methods

Midpoint Euler approximations start as in Euler, but at the *midpoint* of each step, it calculates the slope and redraws the step using the midpoint slope instead of the initial slope. The midpoint Euler method converges considerably more quickly than the original straight-line Euler method.

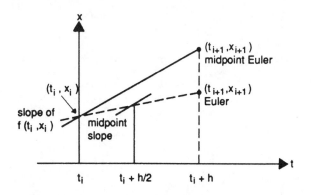

Approximating a solution by the midpoint Euler method.

The reason midpoint Euler works so well is the idea that the slope at the midpoint of an interval is close to the slope of the line between the endpoints.

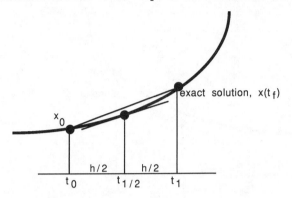

Illustration of midpoint Euler approximation.

Fourth Order Methods

Runge-Kutta (the most common implementation) does quite a bit more "sniffing ahead" and calculating slopes from the beginning, middle, and end of the step. Then it takes a weighted average:

$$m_{RK} = \frac{m_1 + 2m_2 + 2m_3 + m_4}{6} \; ,$$

where m_1 is the initial slope; m_2 is the midpoint slope from a "trial run" with m_1; m_3 is a corrected midpoint slope from using m_2 as a second "trial run"; m_4 is the final slope at the end of a step using m_3.

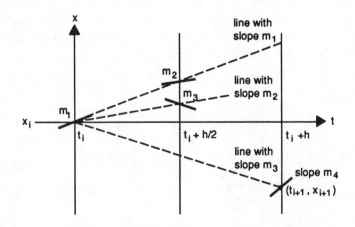

Approximating a solution by the Runge-Kutta method.

The Runge-Kutta method converges considerably faster than either of the Euler methods, and is the default method in the **MacMath** programs. It is probably the most popular numerical method for solving differential equations throughout the world, since the results are usually excellent.

You can experiment with all three methods in the DIFFEQ programs, and you can analyze their differences in the NUMERICAL METHODS program.

Needless to say, these three methods only give a glimpse at the myriad of possibilities for numerical approximation, but they serve well as an introduction. For summary and comparison we list the three methods in the computer language PASCAL. Even if you are not familiar with this programming language, you can read the sequence of equations at the heart of each method.

```
Procedure StepEuler (var t, x, h:real);            Euler's method

Begin
  x := x + h * slope(t, x);
  t := t + h;
end;
```

```
Procedure StepMid(var t, x, h:real);              midpoint Euler

var m1, t1, x1:real;

begin
  t1 := t + h/2; x1 := x + (h/2) * slope(t, x);
  m1 := slope(t1, x1);
  t := t + h;
  x := x + h * m1;
end:
```

```
Procedure StepRK(var t, x, h:real);               Runge–Kutta

var t1, x1, x2, x3, m1, m2, m3, m4, m:real;

begin
  m1 := slope(t, x);
  t1 := t + h/2; x1 := x + m1 * h/2;
  m2 := slope(t1, x1);
  x2 := x + m2 * h/2;
  m3 := slope(t1, x2);
  t := t + h; x3 := x + h * m3;
  m4 := slope(t, x3);
  m := (m1 + 2 * m2 + 2 * m3 + m4)/6;
  x := x + h * m;
end;
```

Table 3.2.3 from p. *123 of Hubbard and West,* Differential *Equations: A Dynamical Systems Approach,* Volume I.

Error, and Order of the Methods

It is an experimental fact that the error in a numerical approximation usually varies as h^p, where p is the order and h is the stepsize. In the case of differential equations (and integrals, by entering $dx/dt = f(t)$), the NUMERICAL METHODS program allows you to explore that fact. This relation of error to order is proven in many texts. For differential equations, see Chapter 3, of Hubbard and West, *Differential Equations: A Dynamical Systems Approach*, Volume I.

The program NUMERICAL METHODS is set up so that you can enter a differential equation $dx/dt = f(t, x)$, an initial time t_0, a final time t_f, an initial position $x_0 = x(t_0)$, and a final position $x_f = x(t_f)$ *if you know the exact value.*

You can further choose to compute approximations, by any of the methods above, for a range of stepsizes, where you bisect the interval t_0 to t_f a certain number n times. Thus

$$h_n = \frac{t_f - t_0}{2^n}$$

is the stepsize using n bisections over a range $n_0 \le n \le n_f$ that you specify.

The computer will compute and display the approximate values $x_n(t_f)$, and the errors *if an exact value x_f was entered.*

Further, if x_f is known, it will display in the "order" column the number k, the approximate order, given by

$$\frac{x_f - x_{n-1}}{x_f - x_n} = 2^k , \qquad \text{or} \qquad k = \log\left(\frac{x_f - x_{n-1}}{x_f - x_n}\right) \Big/ \log 2 .$$

Note that if $x_f - x_n = C\,h^p$, this number will be the theoretical order p, so you can be reasonably confident that the solution is converging properly if the entry is close to the announced order.

If x_f is not known, the entry k in the order column is given by

$$\frac{x_{n-1} - x_{n-2}}{x_n - x_{n-1}} = 2^k , \qquad \text{or} \qquad k = \log\left(\frac{x_{n-1} - x_{n-2}}{x_n - x_{n-1}}\right) \Big/ \log 2 .$$

A computation similar to the above shows that this should still approximate the order.

A further feature of NUMERICAL METHODS allows you to control the precision of the computations. You can modify the number of bits with which the computer calculates, and whether the roundoff is down, up, or round.

This allows the user to study the effect of roundoff error on the precision of the computation.

21

Troubleshooting

Trouble for the Mathematics

There will certainly be occasions when the programs give you false pictures for perfectly good mathematical reasons. You must always justify what you see. You have already seen one instance of a misleading picture in Example 7.1 of Section 7, **DiffEq**, along with a discussion on how to avoid it. The following additional examples are intended to alert you to other possibilities. In each case, try to see what is wrong before you read on to the explanation.

Example 21.1. (*Another example from* DIFFEQ) $\dfrac{dx}{dt} = \sin(t^3 - x^3)$.

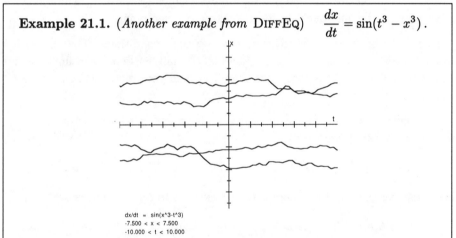

dx/dt = sin(x^3-t^3)
-7.500 < x < 7.500
-10.000 < t < 10.000

This picture is wrong because the solutions are crossing each other, something that usually won't happen. Indeed, if we take a smaller stepsize, the picture straightens out remarkably.

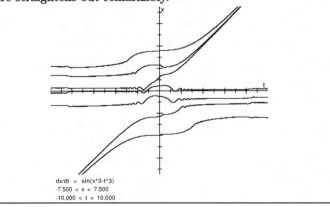

dx/dt = sin(x^3-t^3)
-7.500 < x < 7.500
-10.000 < t < 10.000

Solutions usually don't cross because of *uniqueness*. A more precise statement is the one proved in almost every book on differential equations:

EXISTENCE AND UNIQUENESS THEOREM. *Consider the differential equation $dx/dt = f(t,x)$, with initial condition (t_0, x_0). Then, where f and $\partial f/\partial x$ (partial derivative with respect to the <u>dependent</u> variable) are real, finite, single-valued and continuous, there exists a unique solution to this "initial-value problem".*

The idea of the proof, which is presented in Chapter 4 of Hubbard and West, *Differential Equations: A Dynamical Systems Approach*, Volume I, is to show that between an approximate solution (as calculated by one of our numerical methods) and the actual solution, the error converges to zero as the stepsize gets smaller (limited on the computer by the point where roundoff wreaks havoc).

What is important is that you be able to *use* this theorem and understand what it says with respect to our computer pictures. Existence implies that a trajectory will be drawn; uniqueness implies that trajectories will not cross, since there can be only one solution through any given point.

This theorem states sufficient, but not necessary conditions. That is, all it says is that where the conditions on f and $\partial f/\partial x$ fail, existence and uniqueness cannot be guaranteed; they *may* occur anyway, and your pictures should reflect what actually happens.

You might look at the following two examples where existence and/or uniqueness fail at certain point(s):

$$\text{(a)} \quad \frac{dx}{dt} = 3\,x^{2/3}\,, \qquad\qquad \text{(b)} \quad t\,\frac{dx}{dt} - 3x = 0\,.$$

The same existence and uniqueness theory extends to higher dimensions.

EXISTENCE AND UNIQUENESS THEOREM. *Consider the differential equation*

$$\begin{pmatrix} dx/dt \\ dy/dt \end{pmatrix} = \begin{pmatrix} f(t,x,y) \\ g(t,x,y) \end{pmatrix}, \quad \text{with initial condition} \quad (t_0, x_0, y_0)\,.$$

Then, where f, g, $\partial f/\partial x$, $\partial f/\partial y$, $\partial g/\partial x$ and $\partial g/\partial y$ (partial derivatives with respect to the dependent variables) are real, finite, single-valued and continuous, there exists a unique solution to this "initial-value problem".

Note carefully that a *two*-dimensional picture of txy-space could well have trajectories that appear to cross, whereas the theorem assures us that actually they don't cross in the full *three*-dimensional space.

Uniqueness for an *autonomous* (no explicit dependence on t) two-dimensional differential equation means that trajectories will not cross even in the xy-phase plane. See, for instance, the multisolution pictures in Examples 1.2, 2.1c, 2.4, 2.5 and 2.6. Only at equilibria do phase plane trajectories appear to meet, but notice that they only *approach* the equilibrium and don't actually cross.

The xt and yt pictures show crossings of solutions. In each case, one of the dependent variables is missing, so the graph's ability to separate the solutions in three-dimensional space is lost.

Example 2.7 shows a different sort of breakdown of uniqueness due to the equations not being autonomous.

Smaller stepsize cannot, however, cure a picture over arbitrarily large domains. The approximate solutions nearly always break down, due to instabilities in the approximation, if you look at a sufficiently large domain.

Example 21.2a. The following pictures were obtained in DIFFEQ for $dx/dt = x^2 - t$, for $0 < t < 15$ and stepsize $h = 0.3$. This is Example 2.1 over again, over a larger interval and with a bigger stepsize.

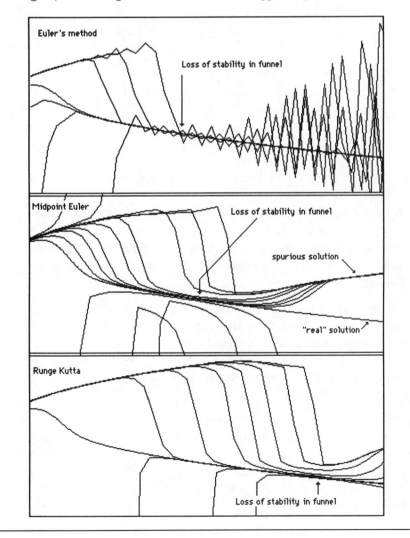

All three approximation methods will eventually break down as t gets large enough, sometimes obviously, and sometimes not so. Even some of the "nice" looking "solutions" are spurious, as can be proved by the following argument (discussed at greater length in Chapter 1 of Hubbard and West, *Differential Equations: A Dynamical Systems Approach*, Volume I).

Example 21.2b.   Recall from Example 2.1 that the default size computer picture for $dx/dt = x^2 - t$ looks like this:

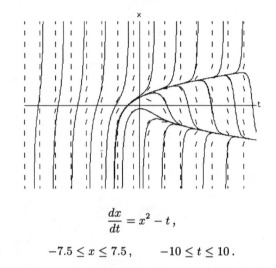

$$\frac{dx}{dt} = x^2 - t\,,$$

$$-7.5 \le x \le 7.5\,, \qquad -10 \le t \le 10\,.$$

By focusing on the isoclines, it is easy to prove that all the solutions in the lower right approach $x = -\sqrt{t}$ as $t \to \infty$, as well as determining where the solutions in the upper right seem to spray apart. It is helpful, in general, to introduce the following terminology in the slope field for a differential equation.

An *upper fence* is a curve (an isocline, in this example) which has slope greater than that of the solutions of the differential equation; a *fence theorem* says that all solutions crossing an upper fence from left to right end up below it forever after.

A *lower fence* is a curve (an isocline, in this example) which has slope less than that of the solutions of the differential equation; a *fence theorem* says that all solutions crossing a lower fence from left to right end up above it forever after.

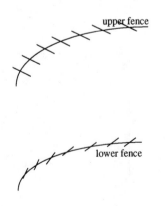

upper fence

lower fence

A *funnel* is composed of an upper fence above a lower fence; a *funnel theorem* says that any solutions which enter the funnel are trapped inside for as long as the funnel lasts.

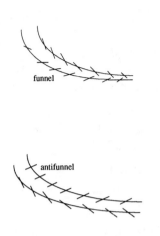

An *antifunnel* is composed of an upper fence below a lower fence, so that solutions keep spraying out when moving from left to right; an *antifunnel theorem* shows that there is always at least one solution staying inside an antifunnel, furthermore, if the antifunnel narrows to zero width, the solution inside is unique.

Some basic isoclines for the equation $dx/dt = x^2 - t$ are as follows, with the slope marks drawn across them. The shaded regions mark a narrowing funnel below (asymptotic to $x = -\sqrt{t}$) and a narrowing antifunnel above (asymptotic to $x = +\sqrt{t}$). This completes a sketch of the promised proof.

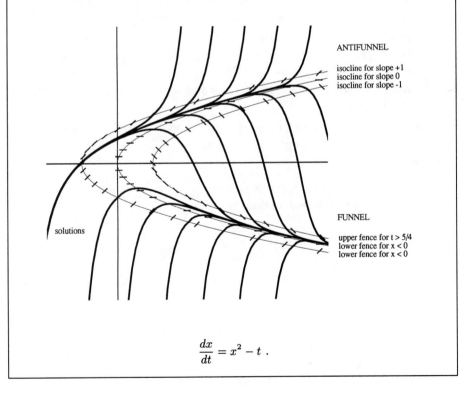

$$\frac{dx}{dt} = x^2 - t \ .$$

Trouble with the Programs

- The first question to ask if you are having any difficulties (especially in printing) is whether you are using Multifinder™— it seems to cause an untold number of problems. Don't, unless you find you can avoid these problems.

- Another potential troublemaker is Gatekeeper™, which can be avoided by going to Gatekeeper™ on the Control Panel, under the menu, and turning on Override .

- If you double-click on a saved file and then get the default equations instead, simply go to the File menu and Open your saved file from within the application.

- If DIFFEQ, 3D VIEWS fails to print all possible graphs, check Page Layout ... under the File menu.

- Whenever solutions or trajectories for differential equations look jagged, try a smaller stepsize.

- Laser printing looks rather ragged for many programs; this is because the graphs are bitmapped. The best you can do for differential equations is to use DIFFEQ, 3D VIEWS, which is the only program giving PostScript™ output.

    For $dx/dt = f(t,x)$, use the txy system with $dy/dt = 1$, and use the xt view (rotate the 3D system to xt view).

    For $dx/dt = f(x,y)$ and $dy/dt = g(x,y)$, use the txy system, and use the xy view (rotate the 3D system to xy view). Unfortunately, you cannot find the 2D singularities and separatrices, however, because $dz/dt = 1 \neq 0$!

- Printing to an Imagewriter II simply does not happen in Draft mode. If you think printing isn't working, check that the Print ... dialog box is set to Faster .

- To get a good electronic copy of a picture, Copy Graph into scrapbook, then paste it into your document *without resizing*.

Index

Absolute value symbol 32
Acceleration 118, 119, 120
Accuracy 27, 114
Accuracy, improving 142, 145, 148
Adding function 41
Adding planets 113
Additive property of topological charge,
    winding number 139
Algorithms, 42, 60, 89, 96, 97
Analytic techniques 5, 51
Analyzer 19-22, 27, 39-46, 51, 66, 85,
    86, 141-143
Analyzing cascades 82, 83
Analyzing cycles 84
Angle, rotation 70, 104
Animation 30, 70, 101
Annihilation of saddles and nodes 62,
    133, 134
Anti-matter 120
Anti-orbit 119
Antifunnel 153
Approximate solution 6, 14, 48, 55, 60,
    68, 69, 144, 150
Approximation method 49, 54, 60
Approximation of a system 128
Approximation, instabilities 151
Approximation, numerical 45, 46, 54,
    141-148
Approximation, piecewise linear 116
Area-preserving iterations 92
Arranging graphs 71
Asymptotes 57, 153
Attraction, basin of 119
Attracting cycles 13, 21, 80, 84-86
Attracting fixed points 20, 78
Attractive force 114, 116
Attractor, strange 74
Autonomous equations 9-17, 28, 59, 60,
    67-69, 131, 150
Averaging methods 142, 144, 146
Axes 33, 68, 70
Axes, rotating 70, 102

Barry Martin mappings 92

Basins 118, 119
Behavior, critical points 85
Behavior, iteration 19-26, 46, 84
Behavior, orbits 19-26, 122, 123
Behavior, phase plane 10, 128, 131
Behavior, planets 114
Bifurcation 59, 61-63, 82, 85, 131,
    133-137
Bifurcation behavior 61, 62, 131-135
Bifurcation diagrams 124-127
Bifurcation locus 62-65
Bifurcations, cascade of 81
Bifurcations, Hopf 62, 137
Bifurcations, saddle-node 62, 133
Bifurcations, sink-source 61, 136
Billiard table 115, 119
Binary planets systems 117, 118
Biological model 2, 3, 65
Birthrate 2
Bisection method 42
Bits, significant 54, 148
Blowup 33, 70, 103
Blowups near singularities 13, 63, 129
Bouncing off walls 119
Bounded orbits 19
Bounds 72, 74, 80, 84, 86, 93, 115
Bounds, for planets 115
Bounds, for axes 33, 68
Bounds, error 54
Box, in diagonal matrix 96
Branching of cascade 82, 85, 86
Breakdown of methods 151

Cardioid 93
Cascade of bifurcations 22, 29, 81-86
Cascade pictures 94
Cascade, shadows in 84
Cascade, skeleton 84
Cascade, universality for 86
Cascade, windows in 84, 86
Cascades, analyzing 82, 83
Center equilibria or singularities 10, 60,
    126
Center of mass 116

Chaos 29, 82, 85, 92, 93
Characteristic polynomials 96, 123
Charge, electrical 114, 119, 120
Charge, topological 137-139
Circuits, nonlinear electric 66, 74
Clearing windows 35
Coalescing nodes and saddles 62, 134
Cobweb diagram 20, 21, 43, 84, 85
Collision of planets 116
Color 34, 40, 88-90
Comparing graphs 42, 52
Comparison of iteration and differential
    equations 121-127
Comparison of numerical methods 57,
    141-147
Competition 65, 80
Complex eigenvalues 96, 97
Complex dynamics 93
Computation speed 108
Computer error 54, 116, 148
Conservation of energy 93, 116
Conservation of momentum 116
Conservation of topological charge
    137-139
Constant coefficients 10
Continuum of cycles 137
Contraction behavior 121, 123, 124
Convergence 45, 46, 85, 96
Convergence, Fourier series 108, 110
Convergence, rate of 144-147
Coordinate display 48, 49, 68, 69
Copy option 36
Crashing program 54, 61, 154
Creep constant 94
Critical points 43, 84-86
Crossing nullclines 131-135
Crossing separatrices 24, 88, 91
Crossing trajectories 10, 15, 16, 149-151
Crowding 65, 80
Cubic polynomials 82, 84, 86
Cursor, disappearing 98
Cycles, in cascades 82-86
Cycles, in Hopf bifurcation 137
Cycles, in Newton's method 86
Cycles, in iteration 21, 23, 46, 82-86
Cycles, limit 13, 61, 62, 65, 66, 138
Cylindrical phase plane 80

Damped motion 11, 14, 15, 66
Deathrate 2
Degenerate quadric surface 101

Degenerate singularities 12, 134
Derivatives 39, 41
Design of planetary systems 117
Determinant of a linearization 61, 62,
    139
Determinant of a matrix 95, 125, 123,
    133
Dewdney 92
Diagonalization of a matrix 95, 101
DiffEq 5, 27, 47-52, 141-147, 149
DiffEq3D 5, 14-17, 28, 67-75, 141-147,
    154
DiffEq, Phase Plane 5, 9-13, 28, 59-66,
    131-136, 144-147
Difference equations 3
Differential equations 1, 5-17, 121-129
Differential equations, autonomous 9,
    59, 60, 67-69, 131, 150
Differential equations, comparison with
    iteration 121-127
Differential equations, first order 47,
    53, 77
Differential equations, linear 10
Differential equations, linearized 13, 61,
    62, 128, 129
Differential equations, nonautonomous
    14-16, 151
Differential equations, nonlinear 12
Differential equations, summary
    bifurcation diagram 126
Differential equations, system 8, 9
Digits, hidden 44
Dimensions 5, 8, 9, 14, 17
Direction diagram, for winding number
    137
Direction field 6, 47, 59
Direction reversal, under gravity
    116-118
Dirichlet kernel 45
Disabled menu items 113
Disappearing cursor 98
Disappearing planets 112, 113, 120
Discrete system 1, 19-26, 117
Display 33, 69, 112
Distortion, of picture 35
Dots in iteration window 73, 81, 87
Dotted trajectories 70, 113
Double flip behavior 26, 88, 122-125
Double potential well 66, 92, 93
Drag coefficient 114
Dripping faucet 74

Driven oscillators 66
Dynamical systems 1-4, 91-94
Dynamical systems, linear 121

Ecology 2-3, 65
Editing graphs 34
Eigendirections 88
EigenFinder 29, 95-99
Eigenvalues 29, 30, 95-97, 101, 102,
    121-125
Eigenvalues, complex 96, 97, 123, 125
Eigenvalues, signs of 124, 125
Eigenvectors 95, 96, 102, 123, 124
Electric circuits, nonlinear 66, 74
Electro-billiards orbit 119
Electromagnetics 111
Electrostatics 30, 114, 118, 119
Ellipsoid 30, 101
Energy 93, 116, 117, 120
Equations 31, 35, 36, 43
Equations, periodic 72, 77
Equilibria 10, 61-63, 69, 88, 89, 121-139
Equilibria, degenerate 12, 134
Equilibria, stability of 11, 78, 121
Error 27, 53
Error analysis 53-57, 148
Error, relation to order 55, 148
Error, roundoff 116, 148
Euler method, modified 92
Euler's method 49, 53-57, 60, 144-147
Even functions 108, 110
Exact error 54, 148
Exchanging singularities 62
Existence theorem 150
Expansion behavior 121, 123, 128
Exponential function 32
Exponentiation symbol 32
Extensions, periodic 110

Failure of existence 150
Failure of Fourier prog 110
Failure of Newton's method 86
Failure of printing 154
Failure of programs 154
Failure of uniqueness 150, 151
Failure to find separatrices 154
Failure to locate singularities 61, 154
Failure to move planets 116
Failure to open file 154
Failure to terminate approximation 108
False pictures 8, 40, 149, 151

Faucet, dripping 74
Feigenbaum point 85
Fence theorem 152
Fences 152, 153
Fertility rate 80
File printer 34, 115
File, failure to open 154
Find option 36
Finding eigenvalues 95, 96, 102
Finding eigenvectors 95, 96, 102
Finding maxima, minima 43
Finding roots, 42
Finding separatrices, failure 154
Finding singularities 60, 69, 89
Finding the period of a function 89
First order differential equations 47, 53,
    77
First order integration methods 144
First order numerical methods 55, 142
Fishing 65, 80
Fixed points 19, 20, 21, 25, 77, 121
Flip behavior 26, 88, 121-125
Flower structure 93
Force constant 114
Forced oscillator 75
Forces 1, 16, 75, 111, 114, 116
Forces, gravitational 120
Forces, periodic 16, 118
Fourier 30, 107-110
Fourier series 45, 46, 107-110
Fourth order methods 55, 143, 146
Foxes 2
Freezing, velocity of a planet 112
Friction 66, 114, 118, 119, 120
Functions, adding 41
Functions, even and odd 108, 110
Functions, graphing 34
Functions, iterating 39, 46
Functions, periodic 72, 77, 78, 110
Funnel theorem 153
Funnels 153

Gatekeeper 154
Geometric interpretation of Jacobi's
    method 102
Gibb's phenomenon 110
Global behavior 25
Graphical iteration 19, 20, 27
Graphs, 34, 35
Graphs, cascade 81
Graphs, of error 55

Graphs, incorrect 8, 40, 149, 151
Graphs, jagged 34, 50, 151, 154
Graphs, period mapping 77, 78
Graphs, printing 71, 154
Gravitational constant 120
Gravity 30, 111, 114, 116-120
Gravity well 116
Gravity, reversal of direction 118
Greek letters 32
Grid points 46
Grid size, changing 104

Harmonic oscillator, damped 66
Harmonics 119
Help 32
Henon mappings 91, 92
Hidden digits 44
Higher order differential equations 8
Homoclinic tangle 25, 88
Hopf bifurcation 62, 137
Hunting 65, 80
Hyperbolic functions 32
Hyperboloid 30, 101

ImagewriterII 154
Imaginary parts of eigenvalues 125
Incorrect graph 8, 40, 149, 151
Index 155
Indifferent fixed point 20
Infinity 36
Information window 68, 72, 112
Initial conditions 6, 27, 54, 68, 77, 88,
    144, 150
Initial state 113
Initial-value problems 150
Instabilities in approximation 151
Integer part 32
Integration 39, 42, 141-143
Interaction between planets 112
Interaction between species 65
Intersecting nullclines 134
Invariance of topological charge 139
Inverse trigonometric functions 32
Invertible maps 92
Irrational rotation number 93
Islands, periods of chains of 91
Isoclines 51, 65, 152, 153
Iterates, marked and unmarked 82
Iterates, numerical list 44
Iterating functions 39, 43, 46, 81
Iteration 1, 3, 19-26, 43, 73, 77

Iteration, finding eigenvalues by 96, 102
Iteration, in cascade 81-86
Iteration orbits 19, 22, 122
Iteration, comparison with differential
    equations 1-4, 26, 121-125
Iteration, graphical 20-24, 122, 123
Iteration, one-dimensional 19-21
Iteration, summary bifurcation diagram
    127
Iteration, two-dimensional 22-26, 87-94,
    121-127
Iterations, area preserving 92

Jacobi's method 29, 30, 95, 96, 99,
    101-103
JacobiDraw 30, 101-105
Jagged trajectories 51, 151, 154
Julia sets 93
Jumps in orbits 118

Kepler 116
Kernel, Dirichlet 45
Kinetic energy 117, 120

Lattice points 118, 119
Layout of page 71
Left-hand method 142
Limit cycles 13, 61, 62, 65, 66, 138
Limiting behavior 133, 153
Linear approximation 55
Linear differential equations 4, 5, 10-12,
    61, 62, 121-126
Linear dynamical systems 121-127
Linear mappings, iterated 25, 121-127
Linear systems 11
Linearization 13, 61, 62, 128, 129,
    133-137
Linearization matrix 128, 129
Linearization, determinant of 61, 62,
    133
Linearization, trace of 61, 62, 136
Lissajous figures 119
Locating roots 85
Locating saddles 92
Locating singularities 12, 28, 59-61,
    67-69, 89, 91, 136, 137
Locus, bifurcation 61-65
Logarithmic function symbol 32
Long range effects 65, 153
Lorenz attractor 74
Lotka 65

Lotka-Volterra 2
Lower fences 152, 153

Mandelbrot set 93
Marked iterates 82
Martin mappings 92
Mass of planets 111-114, 120
Massless planets 118
Matrices 95-105
Maxima 27, 39, 43
Mechanics, classical Newtonian 114
Menu options 36-38
Midpoint Euler method 49, 53-57, 60,
    145-147
Midpoint integration method 143
Mini-cascades 86
Minima 27, 39, 43
Misiurewicz points 85
Modelling, of planets 116, 117
Momentum 116, 117, 119, 120
Multifinder 31, 154

NAN 36
Narrowing funnels, antifunnels 153
Negative eigenvalues 125
Negative mass 114, 120
Negative potential energy 117
Neighborhoods of singularities 137
Neutral cycles 84
Neutral fixed point 20
Newton's law 1, 14
Newton's method 42, 46, 60, 61, 68, 69,
    82, 84, 86, 89
Newton's method, cycling 86
Newtonian mechanics 114
Node sink, source 10, 60
Node, coalescing with saddle 62, 134
Nodes 62, 133, 134, 139
Nonautonomous differential equations
    9, 14, 16, 28, 67, 151
Nonlinear differential equations 4, 5, 11
Nonlinear electric circuits 66, 74
Nonlinear mappings, iterated 12, 26
Nonlinear systems 128, 129
Nonsymmetric matrices 29, 95, 99
Nullclines 131-135
Number length limit 54
Number of bits 148
Number of decimal digits 44
Number of panels for integration 42
Number, planet 112

Number, winding 137, 139
Numerical approximation 141, 142
Numerical integration 42, 141-143
Numerical list of points 69
Numerical methods 5, 53, 141-147
Numerical Methods 27, 53-57
Numerical methods, comparison 57,
    147
Numerical methods, error 55, 148
Numerical methods, order 55, 142, 148
Numerical tunneling 93, 116

Odd functions 108, 110
One-dimensional periodic equations 29,
    77-80
One-two saddle 69
Opening saved files 35, 154
Orbit under iteration 87, 88, 122
Orbits 19-25, 81, 82, 87-89, 122, 123,
    127
Orbits, periodicity 89
Orbits, planets 116, 118
Order of a cycle 84
Order of a Fourier polynomial 108
Order of numerical methods 27, 53, 55,
    142, 148
Oscillations, planets 116, 119
Oscillator, damped harmonic 15, 66
Oscillator, double potential well 66
Oscillator, forced 16, 66, 75

Page layout 71
Painlevé transcendant, first 74
Pair of singularities, creation 133
Parameter, Feigenbaum 85
Parameters 22, 28, 29, 61-63, 80, 133,
    136
Pascal program 147
Pausing 49, 69, 96, 103
Period doubling 85
Period mapping 77-80
Period of a function 89, 108, 110
Period of cycle 86
Periodic equations 28, 29, 72, 73, 77-80
Periodic extensions 110
Periodic forces 16, 118
Periodic motion 1, 2, 14-16
Periodic points 25, 89, 90
Periodic solutions 77, 80
Periodicity of orbits 93
Periodicity, analysis 72, 78, 82-86, 89

Periods of chains of islands 91
Perturbations 51, 65, 80, 84, 91-93, 133, 136
Phase plane 3, 10-13, 59-66, 121-139, 150
Phase plane, cylindrical 80
Pitch 70, 103
Pixels 40, 94
Planetary systems, design of 117
Planets 30, 111-120
Planets, disappearing 112, 113, 120
Planets, orbits of 116
Planets, superimposed 116
Planets, unstable 117, 118
Poincaré sections 67, 72, 73
Point masses 116
Pointwise convergence 110
Pool table 115, 119
Populations 2, 65, 80
Position of a planet 111-113
PostScript™ output 154
Potential energy 117
Potential, double well 66, 92, 93
Predator-prey system 2, 3, 65
Prediction 4, 19, 61, 66, 85, 93
Prediction, weather 74
Preserving area under iteration 92
Principal axes 102
Principal axis theorem 30
Printing 37, 69, 96, 98, 103, 115
Printing graphs 34, 71, 74, 75, 90
Printing, failure 115, 154
Program crashing 54, 61, 154
Programs for numerical methods 147
Programs, pausing 69
Pseudo harmonics 119
Pulses, square 110

QR method 29, 95, 96, 99
Quadratic convergence 96
Quadratic maps 92, 93
Quadratic polynomials 81, 84, 85
Quadric surfaces 30, 101, 102
Qualitative analysis 8

Rabbits 2
Removing functions 41
Removing planets 113
Removing slope marks 49, 60
Repelling cycles 13, 80
Repelling fixed points 20, 78

Repelling forces 118
Repulsion, basin of 118
Resonant motion 11
Reversal of gravity direction 118
Riemann sum 142
Right-hand integration method 142
Rocking three-dimensional graph 28
Roll 70, 103
Roots 42-44, 46, 85
Rössler attractor 74
Rotate to xy-plane 70, 104
Rotating axes 30, 70, 102
Rotation angle 70, 104
Rotation number 93
Rounding 27, 54, 57, 116, 117
Roundoff error 116, 148
Row reduction 97
Rubik's cube 102
Runge-Kutta method 49, 51, 53-57, 60, 77, 146, 147

Saddle 132, 138
Saddle-node bifurcation 62, 63, 133-136
Saddles 10, 60, 62, 121, 122, 124, 126, 127, 132, 138, 139
Saddles, coalescing with nodes 62, 134
Saddles, in iteration 25, 88, 91
Saddles, in three-space 69
Satellites 117, 118
Save option 37
Save screen 34
Saved files, opening 35, 154
Scrapbook 154
Screen save 34
Screen, wrapping 115
Scroll bars, use of 113
Seasonal fertility rate 80
Secant 33
Second order differential equation 1, 8, 9, 11
Second order integration methods 143
Second order numerical methods 145
Seeds 19-23, 42, 87
Separatrices 11, 24, 60, 88-92
Separatrices, criss-crossing 24, 88, 91
Separatrices, failure to draw 89
Separatrices, stability 24, 25
Series, Fourier 45, 46, 107-110
Series, Taylor 45
Shadows in a cascade 84, 85
Sharks 65

Siegel disks 93
Sign of x 32
Significant bits 54
Signs of eigenvalues 124, 125
Simple harmonic motion 119
Simpson's method 46, 143
Simulation 113
Simultaneous graphs 15-17, 71
Singularities 10, 61-63, 69, 88, 89,
    121-129
Singularities, analyzing 67
Singularities, bifurcation behavior
    61-63, 131-137
Singularities, creation of a pair 133
Singularities, degenerate 12, 134
Singularities, double flip 26, 88, 123,
    127
Singularities, failure to locate 61, 154
Singularities, failure to identify 61
Singularities, flip 26, 88, 122, 127
Singularities, linearization around 13,
    128, 129
Singularities, topological charge of
    137
Singularities, type 10, 60, 69, 126,
    127
Singularities, winding number for 137
Sink-source bifurcations 61-63, 136,
    137
Sinks 10, 25, 60, 69, 88, 121-124
Sinks, double flip 123
Sinks, exchanging with sources 62
Sinks, node 60
Sinks, spiral 10, 60, 123, 136
Sinks, weak 136, 137
Sinks, winding number 138
Skeleton of a cascade 84
Slope field 6, 27, 47, 60, 78, 152
Slope field, problems with trajectories
    50
Slope marks, denser 49, 60
Smooth graphs 34, 50, 154
Snooker table 115, 119
Solutions 1, 6, 14, 48
Solutions, approximate 6, 14, 55, 60,
    144, 150
Solutions, behavior 10, 51, 121-126
Solutions, breaking down 51, 149, 151
Solutions, crossing 149, 151
Solutions, false 51, 149, 152
Solutions, jagged 50, 154

Solutions, numerical 27, 53, 54,
    144-147
Solutions, periodic 77, 80
Solutions, trapped 153
Solutions, wrapped 72, 77
Source winding number 138
Sources 10, 25, 60, 69, 88, 121-124
Sources, exchanging with sinks 62
Sources, node 10, 60
Sources, spiral 60, 131, 136
Space bar, use of 49, 69, 91
Species interaction 2, 3, 65, 80
Spectral theorem 30
Speed of rotation 70
Speed of simulation 114
Speeding computation 108
Spin 120
Spiral behavior 121, 122, 125-127
Spiral sinks 10, 60, 123, 136
Spiral sources 60, 131, 136, 137
Spring 1
Spring, damped 14, 15
Spurious solutions 51, 152
Square pulses 110
Square root notation 32
Stable equilibria 11, 78
Stable separatrices 24, 25, 88, 89
Stable system of planets 111
State of a system 113
Step size 7, 50, 51, 53, 55, 93, 114,
    142, 144, 149, 151, 154
Strange attractor 74, 84
String of singularities 135, 139
Structure, flower 93
Subperiods 110
Summary bifurcation diagram
    for differential equations 126
Summary bifurcation diagram
    for iteration 127
Superattracting cycles 84, 85, 86
Superattracting fixed point 20
Superimposed planets 112, 116
Surfaces, quadric 30, 101
Symbols, 32
Symmetric matrices 29, 96, 99, 101
Symmetry, in error analysis 57
Symmetry, of a function 108
Symmetry, with planets 118, 119
System of differential equations 2, 59,
    67, 87
System, planetary 116, 120

Tangential nullclines 134
Tangle, homoclinic 25
Tap, dripping 74
Taylor series 45
Terminal velocity 117, 120
Terminating approximation 108
Terminating drawing 48, 60, 73,
Terminating iteration 73, 88
Three-dimensional autonomous systems
    17, 28, 67-71, 74
Three-dimensional graphs 16, 17, 67-75,
    101-104
Tolerance, for eigenvalues 96, 97, 102,
    104
Tolerance for bisection 42
Tolerance, for periodic points 89
Topological charge 137-139
Torus 115, 118, 119, 120
Trace 95
Trace of a linearization 61, 62, 137
Trace of a matrix 123
Trace-determinant plane 124-127, 133,
    136
Trajectories 9, 28, 59, 60, 67, 68, 72,
    78, 150
Trajectories, behavior 10-13, 121, 122,
    124-126, 131-137
Trajectories, crossing 10, 149, 150
Trajectories, for planets 112, 113
Trajectories, jagged 50, 154
Trajectories, rotating 70, 103
Trajectories, wrapping 72, 73, 78
Transcendant, first Painlevé 74
Trapezoidal method 143
Trapped solutions 153
Trigonometric functions 32
Troubleshooting 50, 149, 151, 154
Truncation 54
Tunneling, numerical 93, 116
Two-dimensional differential
    equations 9-16
Two-dimensional iteration 22-26,
    121-124, 127
Two-dimensional systems,
    converting to 8, 50
Two-one saddle 69
Two-D iterations program 29, 87-94

Two-D periodic equations 72, 73, 75
Types of bifurcations 61-63, 133-137
Types of singularity 10-13, 60, 69, 88,
    121-127

Unbounded universe 115
Unbounded orbits 19, 20, 22
Undo option 37
Uniform convergence 110
Uniqueness in antifunnel 153
Uniqueness theorem 150
Uniqueness, failure 150, 151
Universality of cascade 86
Universe 111, 114, 115
Unmarked iterates 82, 84, 86
Unstable equilibria 11, 78
Unstable planets 117, 118
Unstable separatrices 24, 25, 88, 89
Upper fences 152, 153

Van der Pol's equation 66, 74, 75
Vector field 28, 61, 137
Velocity of a planet 111, 112, 113
Volterra 2, 65

Wallpaper for the mind 92
Weak sinks 61, 62, 136, 137
Weather prediction 74
Weighted average 146
Wells, gravity 116
Wells, potential, double 66, 92, 93
Winding number 137-139
Window, planet information 112
Windows, 33-35
Windows in a cascade 84, 86
Wobbling orbits 116
Wrap around bounds 115, 118
Wrapping trajectories 72, 73, 77, 78

Yaw 70, 103

Zero determinant 133, 136
Zero mass 112
Zero net mass of system 120
Zero trace 137
Zigzagging separatrices 91
Zooming 33, 70, 103

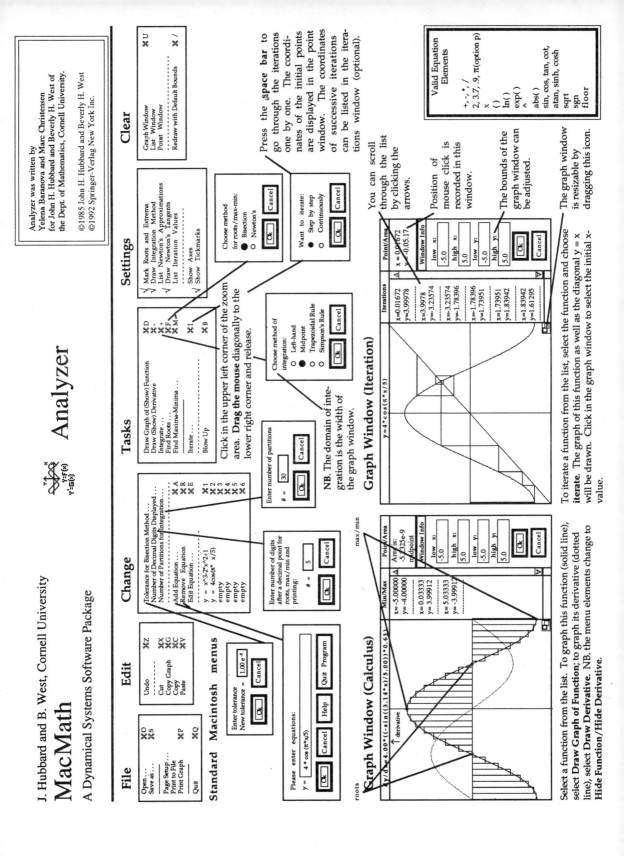

MacMath

J. Hubbard and B. West, Cornell University

A Dynamical Systems Software Package

Analyzer

Analyzer was written by
Yelena Baranova and Marc Christensen
for John H. Hubbard and Beverly H. West of
the Dept. of Mathematics, Cornell University.
©1985 John H. Hubbard and Beverly H. West
©1992 Springer-Verlag New York Inc.

File
Open... ⌘O
Save as... ⌘S
Page Setup...
Print to File
Print Graph ⌘P
Quit ⌘Q

Edit
Undo ⌘Z
Cut ⌘X
Copy Graph ⌘G
Copy ⌘C
Paste ⌘V

Change
Tolerance for Bisection Method...
Number of Decimal Digits Displayed...
Number of Partitions for Integration...
Add Equation... ⌘A
Remove Equation ⌘R
Edit Equation... ⌘E
$y = x^3 - 2x^2 + 1$ ⌘1
$y = 4\cos(\pi x/5)$ ⌘2
empty ⌘3
empty ⌘4
empty ⌘5
empty ⌘6

Tasks
Draw Graph of (Show) Function ⌘D
Draw (Show) Derivative
Integrate... ⌘+
Find Roots... ⌘F
Find Maxima-Minima... ⌘M
Iterate... ⌘I
Blow Up ⌘B

Settings
√ Mark Roots and Extrema
√ Draw Integration Method
√ List Newton's Approximations
√ Draw Newton's Tangents
  List Iteration Values
  Show Axes
√ Show Tickmarks

Clear
Graph Window ⌘U
List Window
Point Window
Redraw with Default Bounds ⌘/

Standard Macintosh menus

Enter tolerance = $1.00\,e^{-3}$
New tolerance = [$1.00\,e^{-3}$]
Ok   Cancel

Please enter equations:
$y =$ [$4 * \cos(\pi x/5)$]
Ok   Cancel   Help   Quit Program

Enter number of partitions
= [30]
Ok   Cancel

Enter number of digits after a decimal point for roots, max/min and printing:
= [5]
Ok   Cancel

Choose method for roots/max-min:
● Bisection
○ Newton's
Ok   Cancel

Want to iterate:
○ Step by step
● Continuously
Ok   Cancel

Choose method of integration:
○ Left-hand
● Midpoint
○ Trapezoidal Rule
○ Simpson's Rule
Ok   Cancel

Valid Equation Elements
+, -, *, /
2, 3.7, .9, π(option p)
x
( )
ln( )
exp( )
^
abs( )
sin, cos, tan, cot,
atan, sinh, cosh
sqrt
sgn
floor

Click in the upper left corner of the zoom area. **Drag the mouse diagonally** to the lower right corner and release.

NB. The domain of integration is the width of the graph window.

Press the **space bar** to go through the iterations one by one. The coordinates of the initial points are displayed in the point window. The coordinates of successive iterations can be listed in the iterations window (optional).

You can scroll through the list by clicking the arrows.

Position of mouse click is recorded in this window.

The bounds of the graph window can be adjusted.

The graph window is resizable by dragging this icon.

Graph Window (Iteration)
$y = 4\cos(\pi x/5)$

Iterations | Point/Area

x=0.01672
y=3.99978
x=3.9978
y=-3.23574
x=-3.23574
y=-1.78396
x=-1.78396
y=1.73951
x=1.73951
y=1.83942
x=1.83942
y=1.61295

Point/Area
x = 0.01672
y = -0.05.17

Window Info
low x: -5.0
high x: 5.0
low y: -5.0
high y: 5.0
Ok   Cancel

To iterate a function from the list, select the function and choose **iterate**. The graph of this function as well as the diagonal y = x will be drawn. Click in the graph window to select the initial x-value.

Graph Window (Calculus)
$y = 4.00*((-\sin((3.14*-x)/5.00))*0.63)$
derivative
roots
max/min

Min/Max | Point/Area

x=-5.00000
y=-4.00000
x=0.03333
y=3.99912
x=5.03333
y=-3.99912

Point/Area
Area is:
-5.325e-9
midpoint

Window Info
low x: -5.0
high x: 5.0
low y: -5.0
high y: 5.0
Ok   Cancel

Select a function from the list. To graph this function (solid line), select **Draw Graph of Function**; to graph its derivative (dotted line), select **Draw Derivative**. NB. the menu elements change to **Hide Function/Hide Derivative**.

MacMath

A Dynamical Systems Software Package

J. Hubbard and B. West, Cornell University

$$\frac{d\mathbf{x}}{dt} = \overset{\cdot}{\underset{\cdot}{\mathbf{x}}} \cdots$$

DiffEq

DiffEq was written by Robert Farrell, Yelena Baranova, and Ben Hinkle for John H. Hubbard and Beverly H. West of the Dept. of Mathematics, Cornell University.

©1985 John H. Hubbard and Beverly H. West
©1992 Springer-Verlag New York Inc.

Standard Macintosh menus

File
Open . . .   ⌘ O
Save as . . .   ⌘ S
Page setup . . .
Print to File
Print Graph   ⌘ P
Quit   ⌘ Q

Edit
Undo   ⌘ Z
Cut   ⌘ X
Copy Graph
Copy   ⌘ C
Paste   ⌘ V

Change
Equation . . .   ⌘ E
Step Size . . .
Method . . .

Task
Blow Up   ⌘ B

Settings
Display Point after Each Step
√ Show Slope Marks
  Show Dense Slope Marks
√ Show Axes
√ Show Tickmarks
  Draw Points Only

Clear
Erase Last Trajectory   ⌘ Y
Erase All Trajectories
Point Window
Return to Default Window Bounds ⌘ U

Please enter equation:

dx/dt =   sin(x+t)*x

[Ok]   [Cancel]   [Help]   [Quit Program]

dv/dt = sin(x+t)*x

Enter step size:

step size =   0.30000

[Ok]   [Cancel]

Choose Method:
○ Euler
○ Midpoint Euler
● Runge-Kutta

[OK]   [Cancel]

Click in the upper left corner of the zoom area. **Drag the mouse** diagonally to the lower right corner and release.

Press the **space bar** to go through the points one by one. Successive coordinates are displayed in the **point window.**

Point
t = -5.45
x = -3.9

Window Info
low t | -10.0
high t | 10.0
low x | -7.5
high x | 7.5
[OK]   [Cancel]

The point window records the **position** of the mouse.

The bounds of the graph window can be adjusted.

The graph window is resizable by dragging this icon.

Click anywhere in the graph window to draw a solution.

Valid Equation Elements

+,-,*,/	Standard arithmetic operations
2, 3.7, .9, π	Numeric values
x	Variable
( )	Parentheses
ln( )	Natural logarithm
exp( )	Exponentiation of e
^	Exponentiation
abs( )	Absolute value
sin, cos, tan, cot,	Trigonometric and hyperbolic
atan, sinh, cosh	trigonometric functions
sqrt	Square root
sgn	Sign of argument (1, 0, or -1)
floor	Step function by truncation

[Ok]

Help Screen

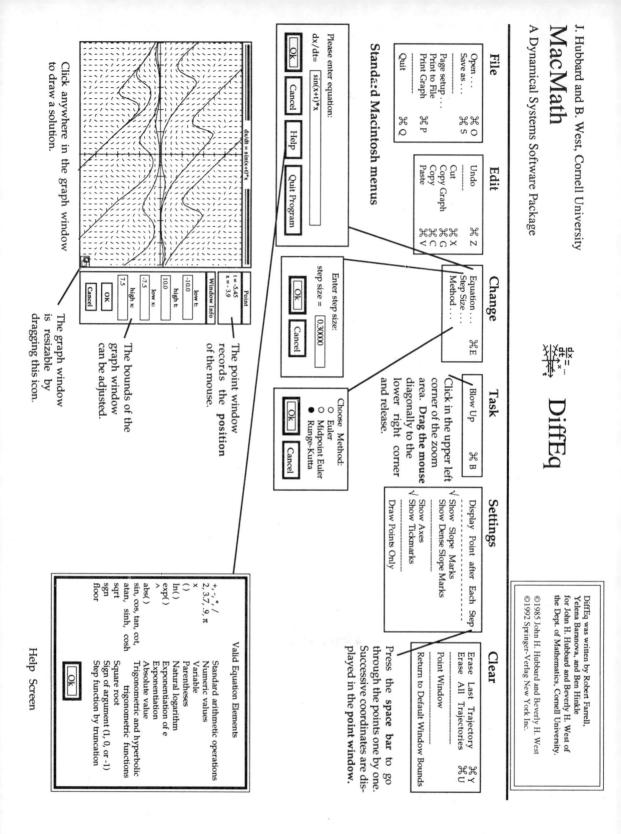

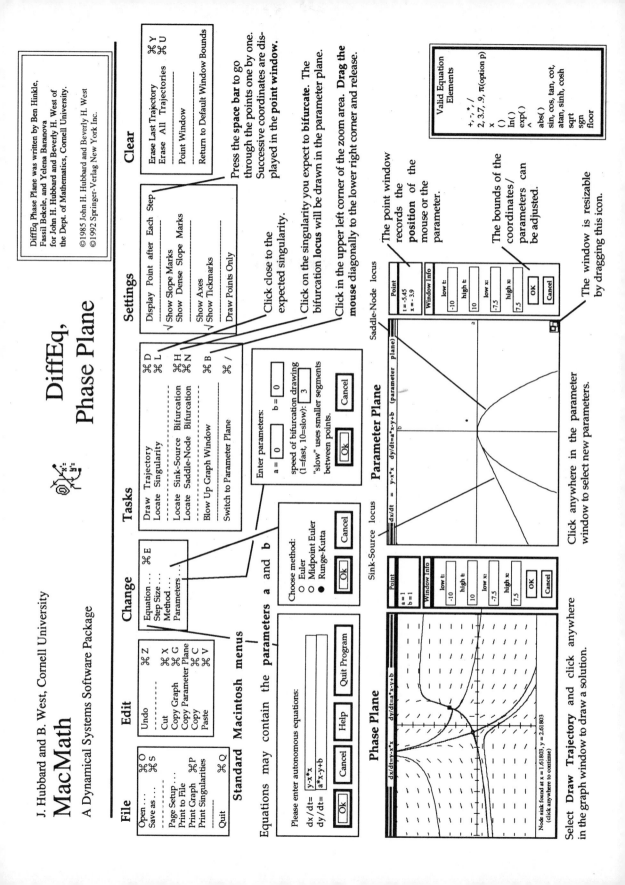

J. Hubbard and B. West, Cornell University

MacMath

A Dynamical Systems Software Package

DiffEq, Phase Plane

DiffEq Phase Plane was written by Ben Hinkle, Fassil Bekele, and Yelena Baranova for John H. Hubbard and Beverly H. West of the Dept. of Mathematics, Cornell University.
©1985 John H. Hubbard and Beverly H. West
©1992 Springer-Verlag New York Inc.

File

Open . . .	⌘O
Save as . . .	⌘S
Page Setup . . .	
Print to File	
Print Graph	⌘P
Print Singularities	
Quit	⌘Q

Edit

Undo	⌘Z
Cut	⌘X
Copy Graph	⌘G
Copy Parameter Plane	
Copy	⌘C
Paste	⌘V

Standard Macintosh menus

Equations may contain the **parameters a and b**

Please enter autonomous equations:

dx/dt = `y-x*x`
dy/dt = `a*x-y+b`

[Ok] [Cancel] [Help] [Quit Program]

Change

Equation . . .	⌘E
Step Size . . .	
Method . . .	
Parameters . . .	

Choose method:
○ Euler
○ Midpoint Euler
● Runge-Kutta

[Ok] [Cancel]

Enter parameters:

a = [0]   b = [0]

speed of bifurcation drawing
(1=fast, 10=slow): [3]
"slow" uses smaller segments between points.

[Ok] [Cancel]

Tasks

Draw Trajectory	⌘D
Locate Singularity	⌘L
Locate Sink-Source Bifurcation	⌘H
Locate Saddle-Node Bifurcation	⌘N
Blow Up Graph Window	⌘B
Switch to Parameter Plane	⌘/

Settings

Display Point after Each Step	
√ Show Slope Marks	
Show Dense Slope Marks	
Show Axes	
√ Show Tickmarks	
Draw Points Only	

Clear

Erase Last Trajectory	⌘Y
Erase All Trajectories	⌘U
Point Window	
Return to Default Window Bounds	

Press the **space bar** to go through the points one by one. Successive coordinates are displayed in the **point window**.

Click close to the expected singularity.

Click on the singularity you expect to **bifurcate**. The bifurcation **locus** will be drawn in the parameter plane.

Click in the upper left corner of the zoom area. **Drag the mouse diagonally** to the lower right corner and release.

Valid Equation Elements

+, -, *, /
2, 3.7, .9, π(option p)
x
( )
ln( )
exp( )
^
abs( )
sin, cos, tan, cot, atan, sinh, cosh
sqrt
sgn
floor

Saddle-Node locus

Point
t = -5.45
x = -3.9

Window Info
low t: [-10]   high t: [10]
low x: [-7.5]   high x: [7.5]
[OK] [Cancel]

The point window records the **position** of the mouse or the parameter.

The bounds of the coordinates / parameters can be adjusted.

The window is resizable by dragging this icon.

Parameter Plane

dx/dt = `y-x*x`   dy/dt = `a*x-y+b`   (parameter plane)

Click anywhere in the parameter window to select new parameters.

Sink-Source locus

Point
a = 1
b = 1

Window Info
low t: [-10]   high t: [10]
low x: [-7.5]   high x: [7.5]
[OK] [Cancel]

Phase Plane

dx/dt=`y-x*x`   dy/dt=`a*x-y+b`

Node sink found at x = 1.61803 , y = 2.61803
(click anywhere to continue)

Select **Draw Trajectory** and click anywhere in the graph window to draw a solution.

J. Hubbard and B. West, Cornell University

MacMath
A Dynamical Systems Software Package

DiffEq
3D Views

DiffEq, 3D Views was written by Ben Hinkle for John H. Hubbard and Beverly H. West of the Dept. of Mathematics, Cornell University.

©1985 John H. Hubbard and Beverly H. West
©1992 Springer-Verlag New York Inc.

Standard Macintosh menus

File
Open... ⌘O
Save as... ⌘S

Page Setup...
Page Layout...
Print to File

Page Setup...
Print Graphs ⌘P
Print Last Trajectory
Print Singularities

Quit ⌘Q

Edit
Undo ⌘Z

Cut ⌘X
Copy ⌘C
Copy Graph
Paste ⌘V

Page Layout
- 1) 3-d space
- 2) x-y plane
- 3) y-z plane
- 4) x-z plane
- 5) x-t plane
- 6) y-t plane
- 7) z-t plane
□ Square Boxes

[Cancel] [Ok]

Only on formatted printout can you see xt, yt, zt graphs for xyz system.

Change
Equations...
Step Size...
Method...
Rotation Angle...
Reverse Rotation

⌘E

⌘/

Please enter autonomous equations:

$dx/dt = f(x,y,z) = $ y
$dy/dt = g(x,y,z) = $ -x
$dz/dt = h(x,y,z) = $ 1

[Ok] [Switch System] [Quit] [Help]

System in x, y, z

Please enter autonomous equations:

$dx/dt = f(x,y,t) = $ y
$dy/dt = g(x,y,t) = $ - x/5 + cos (t) /10
□ System is periodic in time   Period: 2π

[Ok] [Switch System] [Quit] [Help]

$dx/dt = y, dy/dt = -x, dz/dt = 1$

Window Info
Scroll to xy, xz or yz views

	x: 0	-5 to 5
y: 2	-5 to 5
t: 0	0 to 50

[Solve] [Set Bounds]

Coordinates for start of solution can be entered numerically here; then click **Solve**.

Click when you have entered desired bounds in all six boxes.

Tasks
Draw Trajectory ⌘D
Locate Singularity ⌘L

Pitch (Horizontal Axis of Screen) ⌘1
Yaw (Vertical Axis of Screen) ⌘2
Roll (Perpendicular to Screen) ⌘3

Rock Graph

Center Graph at Origin
Move Away from Graph
Move Towards Graph
Rotate to x-y plane ⌘4
Rotate to x-z plane ⌘5
Rotate to y-z plane ⌘6

Choose Method:
○ Euler
● Midpoint Euler
○ Runge-Kutta

[Ok] [Cancel]

Settings
√ Quick Rotate
Step-by-Step Drawing
Draw Points Only
Draw Periodic Points Only
Draw Reference Rectangles

Rotate the graph in any of three directions using the **Rotation Angle** set under the **Change Menu**. To continue to rotate in the same direction, hold down a ⌘-number combination.

To animate a rotation, choose **Rock Graph**. Then keep the mouse held down until the graph has rotated through enough steps. Release the mouse button, and the graph will rock back and forth until you click again. To speed (slow) the rocking motion, raise (lower) the **Rotation Angle** under the **Change Menu**.

Clear
Erase Last Trajectory ⌘Y
Erase All Trajectories
Return to Default View ⌘U

Periodic System in x, y

Enter step size:
step size = 0.3000

[Ok] [Cancel]

Enter rotation angle:
angle (in degrees) = 15

[Ok] [Cancel]

$dx/dt = y, dy/dt = -x/5 - cos(t)/10$

reference rectangles
wrapped trajectory in x,y,t-space
t=0
t = period

Poincaré Section

	x: 0.509	-5 to 5
y: 0.108	-5 to 5
t: 0.000	0 to 6.28

[Solve] [Set Bounds]

period

Choose Locate Singularity from Task menu, then click on graph near where you expect to find one. Type of singularity labelled here, beneath its coordinates. The type is labelled by number on the 3D graph.

Locate Singularity from the Task menu, then click on graph near where you expect to find one.

Valid Equation Elements
+, -, *, /
2, 3.7, .9, π(option p)
x
ln( )
exp( )
^
abs( )
sin, cos, tan, cot,
atan, sinh, cosh
sqrt
sgn
floor

1: sink
2: 2-1 saddle
3: 1-2 saddle
4: source

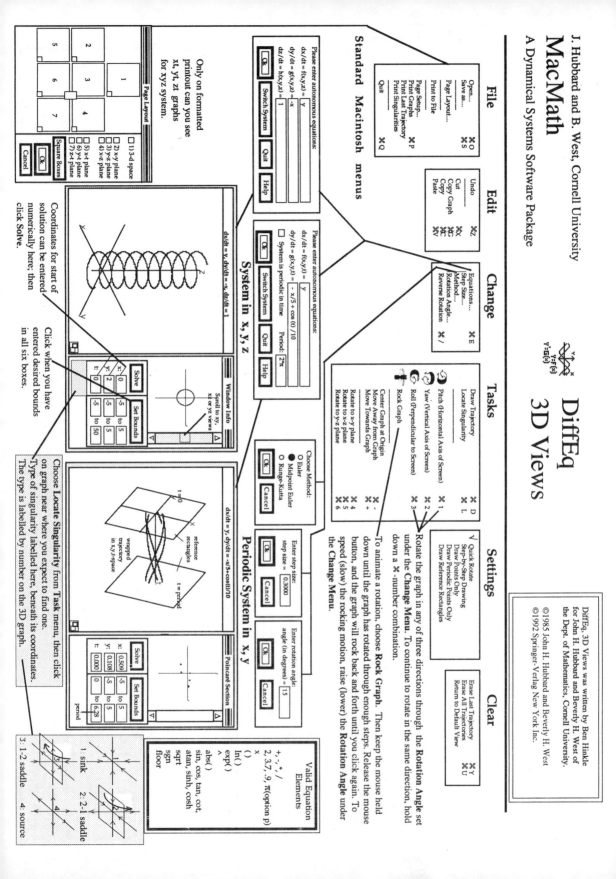

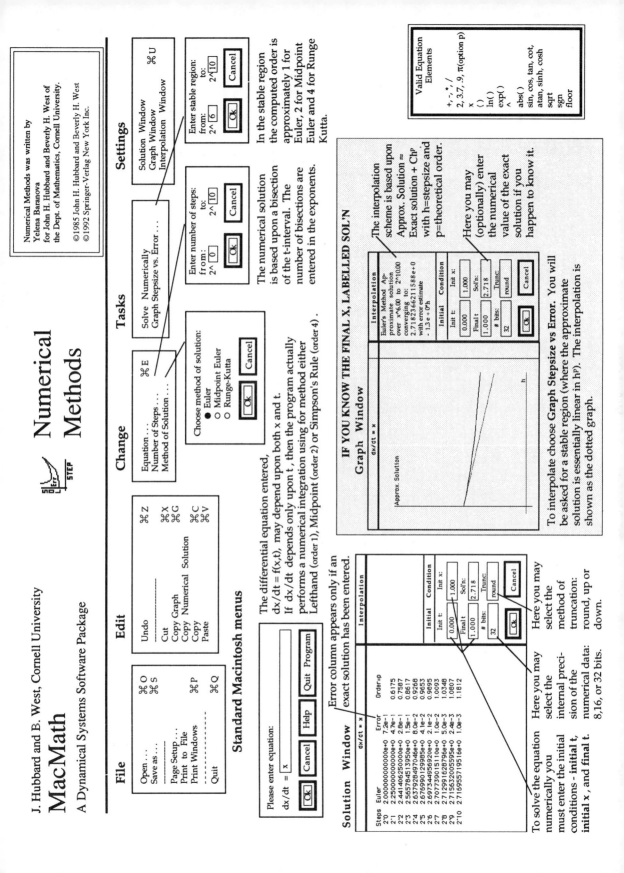

J. Hubbard and B. West, Cornell University

MacMath

A Dynamical Systems Software Package

Numerical Methods

Numerical Methods was written by Yelena Baranova for John H. Hubbard and Beverly H. West of the Dept. of Mathematics, Cornell University.
©1985 John H. Hubbard and Beverly H. West
©1992 Springer-Verlag New York Inc.

File

Open . . .	⌘O
Save as . . .	⌘S

Page Setup . . .	
Print to File	
Print Windows	⌘P

Quit	⌘Q

Edit

Undo	⌘Z

Cut	⌘X
Copy Graph	⌘G
Copy Numerical Solution	
Copy	⌘C
Paste	⌘V

Standard Macintosh menus

Change

Equation . . .	⌘E
Number of Steps . . .	
Method of Solution . . .	

Tasks

Solve Numerically
Graph Stepsize vs. Error . . .

Settings

Solution Window	
Graph Window	⌘U
Interpolation Window	

Choose method of solution:
- ● Euler
- ○ Midpoint Euler
- ○ Runge-Kutta

[Ok] [Cancel]

Enter number of steps:
from: to:
2^ [0]   2^[10]
[Ok] [Cancel]

Enter stable region:
from: to:
2^[6]   2^[10]
[Ok] [Cancel]

Please enter equation:
dx/dt = [x]
[Ok] [Cancel] [Help] [Quit Program]

The differential equation entered, dx/dt = f(x,t), may depend upon both x and t. If dx/dt depends only upon t, then the program actually performs a numerical integration using for method either Lefthand (order 1), Midpoint (order 2) or Simpson's Rule (order 4).

The numerical solution is based upon a bisection of the t-interval. The number of bisections are entered in the exponents.

In the stable region the computed order is approximately 1 for Euler, 2 for Midpoint Euler and 4 for Runge Kutta.

The interpolation scheme is based upon Approx. Solution ≈ Exact solution + Ch^p with h=stepsize and p=theoretical order.

Here you may (optionally) enter the numerical value of the exact solution if you happen to know it.

Solution Window

dx/dt = x

Steps	Euler	Error	Order-p
2^0	2.0000000000000e+0	7.2e-1	
2^1	2.2500000000000e+0	4.7e-1	0.6175
2^2	2.4414062500000e+0	2.6e-1	0.7587
2^3	2.5655784513950e+0	1.5e-1	0.8617
2^4	2.6379284970460e+0	8.0e-2	0.9268
2^5	2.6769901299850e+0	4.1e-2	0.9653
2^6	2.6973449569200e+0	2.1e-2	0.9895
2^7	2.7077390151100e+0	1.0e-2	1.0093
2^8	2.7129916287960e+0	5.0e-3	1.0348
2^9	2.7156320055950e+0	2.4e-3	1.0807
2^{10}	2.7169555719516e+0	1.0e-3	1.1812

Interpolation

Initial	Condition	
Init t: [0.000]	Init x: [1.000]	
Final t [1.000]	Soln: [2.718]	
# bits: [32]	Trunc: [round]	

[Ok] [Cancel]

To solve the equation numerically you must enter the initial conditions - initial t, initial x, and final t.

Here you may select the internal precision of the numerical data: 8,16, or 32 bits.

Here you may select the method of truncation: round, up or down.

Error column appears only if an exact solution has been entered.

IF YOU KNOW THE FINAL X, LABELLED SOL'N

Graph Window

dx/dt = x

Approx. Solution

h

Interpolation

Euler's Method Approximate solution over x^6.00 to 2^10.00 converging to: 2.718366211588e+0 with error estimate -1.3 e+0^h

Initial	Condition	
Init t: [0.000]	Init x: [1.000]	
Final t [1.000]	Soln: [2.718]	
# bits: [32]	Trunc: [round]	

[Ok] [Cancel]

To interpolate choose Graph Stepsize vs Error. You will be asked for a stable region (where the approximate solution is essentially linear in h^p). The interpolation is shown as the dotted graph.

Valid Equation Elements

+,-,*,/
2, 3.7, .9, π(option p)
x
( )
ln( )
exp( )
^
abs( )
sin, cos, tan, cot, atan, sinh, cosh
sqrt
sgn
floor

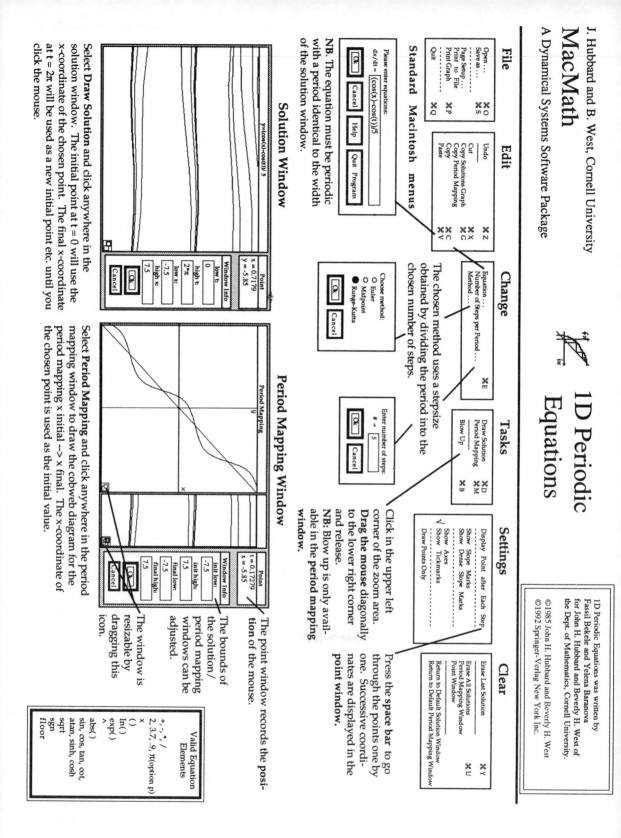

J. Hubbard and B. West, Cornell University

MacMath
A Dynamical Systems Software Package

1D Periodic Equations

1D Periodic Equations was written by Fassil Bekele and Yelena Baranova for John H. Hubbard and Beverly H. West of the Dept. of Mathematics, Cornell University.
©1985 John H. Hubbard and Beverly H. West
©1992 Springer-Verlag New York Inc.

File
Open...	⌘O
Save as...	⌘S
Cut	
Page Setup...	
Print to File	
Print Graph	⌘P
Quit	⌘Q

Standard Macintosh menus

Edit
Undo	⌘Z
Cut	⌘X
Copy Solutions Graph	⌘G
Copy Period Mapping	
Copy	⌘C
Paste	⌘V
Quit Program	

Please enter equations:

dx/dt = $(\cos(x)-\cos(t))/5$

OK Cancel Help Quit Program

NB. The equation must be periodic with a period identical to the width of the solution window.

Change
Equation...	⌘E
Number of Steps per Period...	
Method...	

The chosen method uses a stepsize obtained by dividing the period into the chosen number of steps.

Choose method:
○ Euler
○ Midpoint
● Runge-Kutta
OK Cancel

Tasks
Draw Solution	⌘D
Period Mapping	⌘M
Blow Up	⌘B

Enter number of steps:
= 5
OK Cancel

Settings
Display Point after Each Step
Show Slope Marks
Show Dense Slope Marks
√ Show Axes
√ Show Tickmarks
Draw Points Only

Clear
Erase Last Solution	⌘Y
Erase All Solutions	
Period Mapping Window	
Point Window	
Return to Default Solution Window	
Return to Default Period Mapping Window	⌘U

Solution Window
y=(cos(x)-cos(t))/5

Point
x = 0.7179
y = -5.85

Window Info
low t: 0
high t: 2*π
low x: -7.5
high x: 7.5
OK Cancel

Select **Draw Solution** and click anywhere in the solution window. The initial point at t = 0 will use the x-coordinate of the chosen point. The final x-coordinate at t = 2π will be used as a new initial point etc. until you click the mouse.

Period Mapping Window
Period Mapping

Point
t = 0.17279
x = -5.85

Window Info
init low: -7.5
init high: 7.5
final low: -7.5
final high: 7.5
OK Cancel

Select **Period Mapping** and click anywhere in the period mapping window to draw the cobweb diagram for the period mapping x initial --> x final. The x-coordinate of the chosen point is used as the initial value.

Select **Period Mapping** and click anywhere in the period mapping window. The bounds of the solution / period mapping windows can be adjusted.

The bounds of the solution / period mapping windows can be adjusted.

The window is resizable by dragging this icon.

The point window records the position of the mouse.

Click in the upper left corner of the zoom area. **Drag the mouse diagonally** to the lower right corner and release.
NB: Blow up is only available in the **period mapping window.**

Press the **space bar** to go through the points one by one. Successive coordinates are displayed in the **point window.**

Valid Equation Elements
+, -, *, /
2, 3.7, .9, π(option p)
x
( )
ln( )
exp( )
^
abs( )
sin, cos, tan, cot,
atan, sinh, cosh
sqrt
sgn
floor

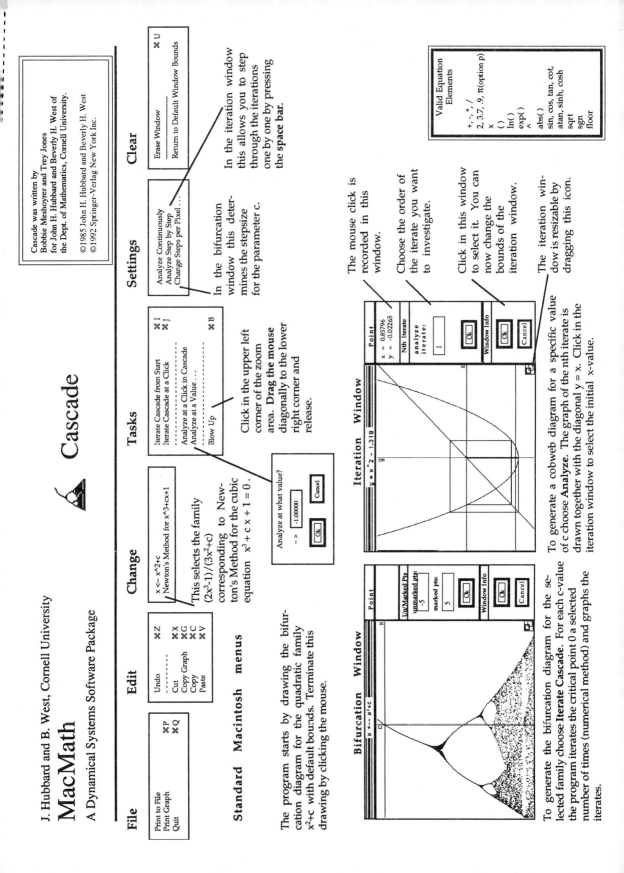

J. Hubbard and B. West, Cornell University

MacMath
A Dynamical Systems Software Package

Cascade

Cascade was written by
Bobbie Meshoyrer and Trey Jones
for John H. Hubbard and Beverly H. West
for John H. Hubbard and Beverly H. West of
the Dept. of Mathematics, Cornell University.

©1985 John H. Hubbard and Beverly H. West
©1992 Springer-Verlag New York Inc.

File

Print to File ⌘P
Print Graph
Quit ⌘Q

Standard Macintosh menus

The program starts by drawing the bifurcation diagram for the quadratic family $x^2 + c$ with default bounds. Terminate this drawing by clicking the mouse.

Edit

Undo ⌘Z

Cut ⌘X
Copy Graph ⌘G
Copy ⌘C
Paste ⌘V

Change

x <- x^2+c
Newton's Method for x^3+cx+1

This selects the family $(2x^3-1)/(3x^2+c)$ corresponding to Newton's Method for the cubic equation $x^3 + c x + 1 = 0$.

Analyze at what value?

--> -1.00000

Ok   Cancel

Tasks

Iterate Cascade from Start ⌘I
Iterate Cascade at a Click ⌘J

Analyze at a Click in Cascade
Analyze at a Value . . .

Blow Up ⌘B

Click in the upper left corner of the zoom area. **Drag the mouse** diagonally to the lower right corner and release.

Settings

Analyze Continuously
Analyze Step by Step
Change Steps per Pixel. . .

In the bifurcation window this determines the stepsize for the parameter c.

Clear

Erase Window ⌘U
Return to Default Window Bounds

In the iteration window this allows you to step through the iterations one by one by pressing the **space bar**.

Bifurcation Window

x <-- x^2+c

Un/Marked Pts
unmarked pts:
-5
marked pts:
5
Ok
Window Info
Ok   Cancel

To generate the bifurcation diagram for the selected family choose **Iterate Cascade**. For each c-value the program iterates the critical point 0 a selected number of times (numerical method) and graphs the iterates.

Iteration Window

y = x ^2 - 1.319

Point
x = 0.85796
y = -0.02265
Nth Iterate
analyze iterate:
1
Ok
Window Info
Ok   Cancel

The mouse click is recorded in this window.

Choose the order of the iterate you want to investigate.

Click in this window to select it. You can now change the bounds of the iteration window.

The iteration window is resizable by dragging this icon.

To generate a cobweb diagram for a specific value of c choose **Analyze**. The graph of the nth iterate is drawn together with the diagonal y = x. Click in the iteration window to select the initial x-value.

Valid Equation Elements

+, -, *, /
2, 3, 7, .9, π(option p)
x
( )
ln( )
exp( )
^
abs( )
sin, cos, tan, cot,
atan, sinh, cosh
sqrt
sgn
floor

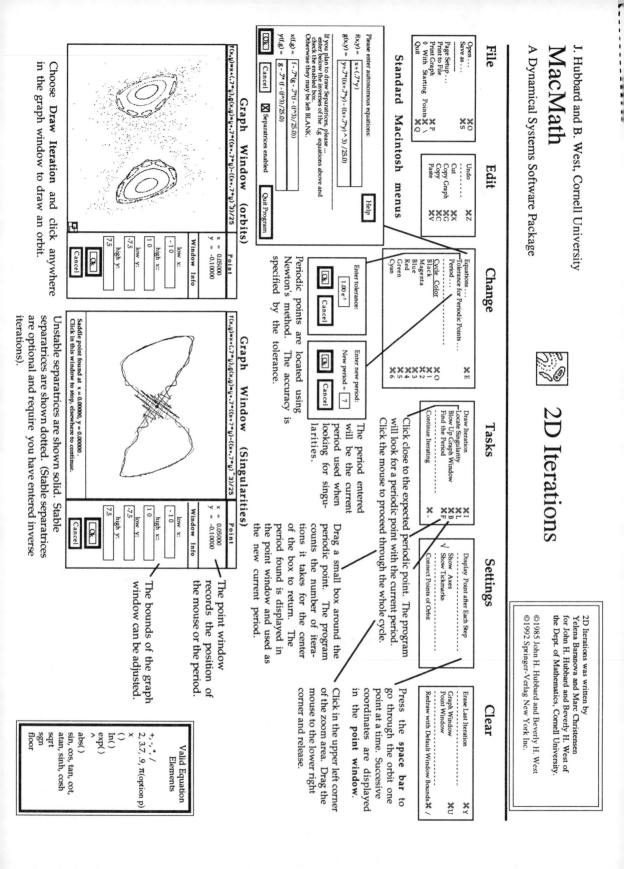

J. Hubbard and B. West, Cornell University

MacMath

A Dynamical Systems Software Package

2D Iterations

2D Iterations was written by Yelena Baranova and Marc Christensen for John H. Hubbard and Beverly H. West of the Dept. of Mathematics, Cornell University.

File

Open... ⌘O
Save as... ⌘S

Page Setup...
Print to File
Print Graph ⌘P
◇ With Starting Points ⌘ \
Quit ⌘Q

Edit

Undo ⌘Z

Cut ⌘X
Copy Graph ⌘G
Copy ⌘C
Paste ⌘V

Standard Macintosh menus

Equations dialog

Please enter autonomous equations:

$f(x,y) = x+(.7*y)$

$g(x,y) = y+.7*(x+.7*y)-((x+.7*y)^3)/25.0)$

If you plan to draw Separatrices, please enter below the inverse of the f,g equations above and check the enabled box. Otherwise they may be left BLANK.

$x(f,g) = f-.7*(g-.7*(f-(f^3)/25.0))$

$y(f,g) = g-.7*(f-(f^3)/25.0)$

[OK] ☒ Separatrices enabled [Cancel]   [Help]   [Quit Program]

Change

Equations...
Tolerance for Periodic Points...
Period...

Cycle Color ⌘E
Black ⌘0
Magenta ⌘1
Blue ⌘2
Red ⌘3
Green ⌘4
Cyan ⌘5
  ⌘6

Enter tolerance: 1.00 e⁵ [OK] [Cancel]

Enter new period: New period = 7 [OK] [Cancel]

Periodic points are located using Newton's method. The accuracy is specified by the tolerance.

The period entered will be the current period used when looking for singularities.

Tasks

Draw Iteration ⌘I
Locate Singularity ⌘L
Blow Up Graph Window ⌘B
Find the Period ⌘F
Continue Iterating ⌘-

Click close to the expected periodic point. The program will look for a periodic point with the current period. Click the mouse to proceed through the whole cycle.

Drag a small box around the periodic point. The program counts the number of iterations it takes for the center of the box to return. The period found is displayed in the point window and used as the new current period.

Settings

Display Point after Each Step
Show Axes
√ Show Tickmarks
Connect Points of Orbit

Press the space bar to go through the orbit one point at a time. Successive coordinates are displayed in the point window.

Click in the upper left corner of the zoom area. Drag the mouse to the lower right corner and release.

Clear

Erase Last Iteration ⌘Y
Graph Window
Point Window ⌘U
Redraw with Default Window Bounds ⌘/

Graph Window (orbits)

f(x,y)=x+(.7*y),g(x,y)=y+.7*(x+.7*y)-((x+.7*y)^3)/25

Window Info   Point
x = 0.05000
y = -0.10000
low x: -10   high x: 10
low y: -7.5   high y: 7.5
[Ok] [Cancel]

Choose **Draw Iteration** and click anywhere in the graph window to draw an orbit.

Graph Window (Singularities)

f(x,y)=x+(.7*y),g(x,y)=y+.7*(x+.7*y)-((x+.7*y)^3)/25

Saddle point found at x = 0.00000, y = 0.00000. Click in this window to stop, elsewhere to continue.

Window Info   Point
x = 0.05000
y = -0.10000
low x: -10   high x: 10
low y: -7.5   high y: 7.5
[Ok] [Cancel]

The point window records the position of the mouse or the period.

The bounds of the graph window can be adjusted.

Unstable separatrices are shown solid. Stable separatrices are shown dotted. (Stable separatrices are optional and require you to have entered inverse iterations).

Valid Equation Elements

+, -, *, /
2, 3.7, .9, π(option p)
x
( )
ln( )
exp( )
^
abs( )
sin, cos, tan, cot,
atan, sinh, cosh
sqrt
sgn
floor

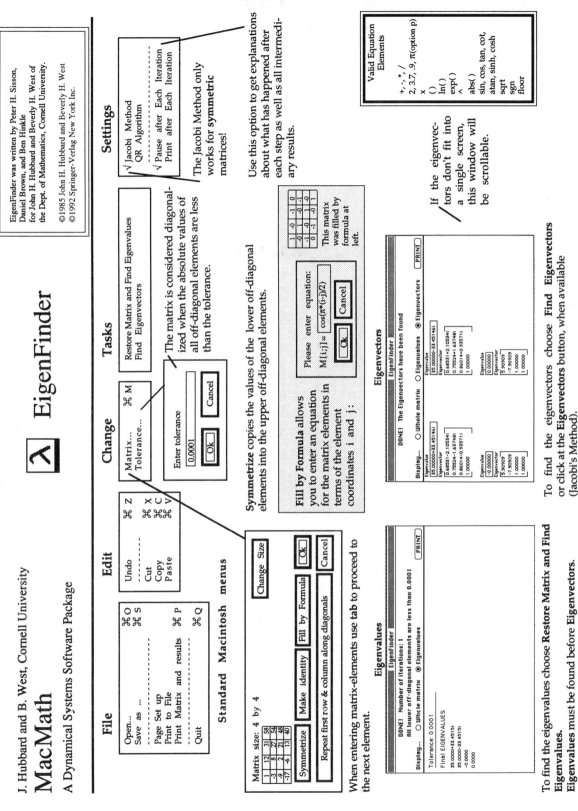

J. Hubbard and B. West, Cornell University

MacMath

A Dynamical Systems Software Package

JacobiDraw was written by
Peter Sisson, Trey Jones, and Ben Hinkle
for John H. Hubbard and Beverly H. West of
the Dept. of Mathematics, Cornell University.

JacobiDraw

File

Open . . .	⌘O
Save as . . .	⌘S
Page Setup . . .	
Print to File	
Print Graph	⌘P
Quit	⌘Q

Edit

Undo	⌘Z
Cut	⌘X
Copy Graph	⌘G
Copy	⌘C
Paste	⌘V

Standard Macintosh menus

Change

Matrix . . .	⌘M
Tolerance . . .	
Rotation Angle . . .	
Grid Size . . .	
Reverse Rotation Direction	⌘ /

Enter a symmetric matrix:

```
  3   -1
 -1    2
  2    5
```

[Ok]   [Cancel]

The matrix is considered diagonalized when the absolute values of all off-diagonal elements are less than the tolerance.

Enter tolerance:
tolerance = 0.0001

[Ok]   [Cancel]

The quadric surface associated with the symmetric matrix is drawn in the graph window.

Enter rotation angle:
angle = 10.0 °

[Ok]   [Cancel]

Tasks

Find Eigenvalues	⌘F
Reset Matrix	⌘T
- - - - - - - -	
Pitch (Horizontal Axis of Screen)	⌘1
Yaw (Vertical Axis of Screen)	⌘2
Roll (Perpendicular to Screen)	⌘3
- - - - - - - -	
Move Away from Graph	⌘-
Move Towards Graph	⌘+
- - - - - - - -	
Rotate to x-y Plane	⌘4
Rotate to x-z Plane	⌘5
Rotate to y-z Plane	⌘6
Return to Default View	

Enter gridsize for drawing surface

Number of Slices: 6
Points per Slice: 12

[Ok]   [Cancel]

Raise for more slices.
Raise for better resolution.

Settings

Draw Half of Surface	
Pause after Each Iteration/	
Print after Each Iteration	

Press **space bar** to continue after pause.

To rotate "continuously" keep the command key pressed down.

For all surfaces but ellipsoids, the surface is shown in slices to improve visualization.
The numbers give a rough measure of the possibilities. (Only one quadrant of each slice is computed; symmetry is used to draw the rest.)

Example: sliced Hyperboloid.

Graph Window during Iteration

JacobiDraw

Status

Matrix during Iteration 1:

```
 3.0000  -1.0000   2.0000
-1.0000   2.0000  -2.0000
 2.0000  -2.0000   5.0000
         ↓
 1.7639   0.2208  -0.0000
 0.2208   2.0000  -2.2270
 0.0000  -2.2270   6.2361
```

Iteration 1: Rotating −31.717 degrees in the XZ plane

The quadric surface associated with the symmetric matrix is drawn in the graph window.

Choose Find Eigenvalues to start rotating the coordinate system around one of its axes to remove an off-diagonal matrix element; **hit space bar** to see next iteration.

The quadric surface cuts the plane of rotation in a conic section; the coordinate axes rotate to align with the symmetry axes of this conic section.

Eigenvalues and Eigenvectors

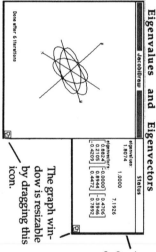

JacobiDraw

Status

```
eigenvalue:
 1.8074       1.0000        7.1926

eigenvectors:
 0.8824  -0.0000   0.4706
 0.1051   0.9744  -0.3946
-0.0209   0.4471   0.7894
```

Done after 6 iterations

The graph window is resizable by dragging this icon.

When finished the status window contains information about eigenvalues and eigenvectors.

The axes of the coordinate system end up aligned with the symmetry axes of the quadric surface (corresponding to the eigendirections). You can rotate to each of the new coordinate planes to check this.

J. Hubbard and B. West, Cornell University

MacMath

A Dynamical Systems Software Package

Fourier Series

File

Open …	⌘O
Save as …	⌘S
Page Setup …	
Print to File	
Print Graph	⌘P
Quit	⌘Q

Edit

Undo	⌘Z
Cut	⌘X
Copy Graph	⌘G
Copy	⌘C
Paste	⌘V

Change

Function by Formula …	⌘E
Function by Cursor	
Period …	

Tasks

Plot Series …	
Blow Up Graph Window	⌘B

Settings

Show Axes
Show Tickmarks

Clear

Entire Graph Window	⌘U
Restore Function	
Order Window	
Point Window	
Return to Default Window Bounds	

Standard Macintosh menus

Please enter equation:

y = x^2/5

Ok   Cancel   Help   Quit Program

To start the program you have to select
either **Function by Formula** or **Function
by Cursor** from the Change menu.

Enter new period:

New period = 6.2832

Ok   Cancel

Only available
when you enter
by formula!

Click in the upper left corner of the zoom area.
Drag Mouse diagonally to the lower right corner
and release. Blow up is only available when you
enter by formula.

The function is:
● Even
○ Odd
○ Neither

Ok   Cancel

Once the function has a symmetry you can cut down computations by clicking the symmetry. If you select a symmetry, say
even, Fourier series will approximate the even part of your
function:

$$f(x) = \sum a_n \cos(nx) + \sum b_n \sin(nx)$$

even part   odd part

Graph Window (Enter by Formula)

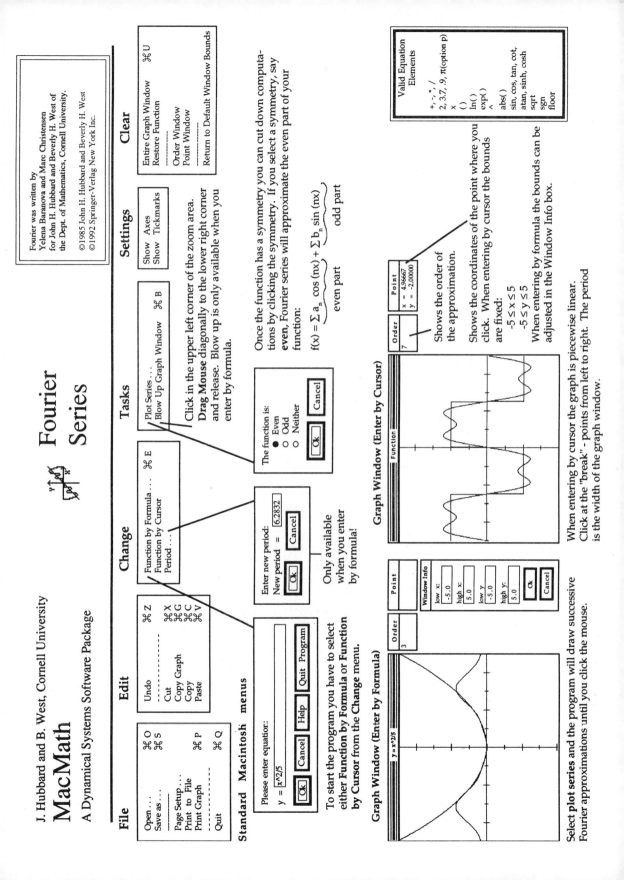

Order   3

y = x^2/5

Point

Window Info

low x:	-5.0
high x:	5.0
low y:	-5.0
high y:	5.0

Ok   Cancel

Select plot series and the program will draw successive
Fourier approximations until you click the mouse.

Graph Window (Enter by Cursor)

Order   7

Function

Point
x = 4.96667
y = -2.00000

Shows the order of
the approximation.

Shows the coordinates of the point where you
click. When entering by cursor the bounds
are fixed:

-5 ≤ x ≤ 5
-5 ≤ y ≤ 5

When entering by formula the bounds can be
adjusted in the Window Info box.

When entering by cursor the graph is piecewise linear.
Click at the "break" - points from left to right. The period
is the width of the graph window.

**Valid Equation
Elements**

+, -, *, /
2, 3.7, .9, π(option p)
x
( )
ln( )
exp( )
^
abs( )
sin, cos, tan, cot,
atan, sinh, cosh
sqrt
sgn
floor

J. Hubbard and B. West, Cornell University

MacMath

A Dynamical Systems Software Package

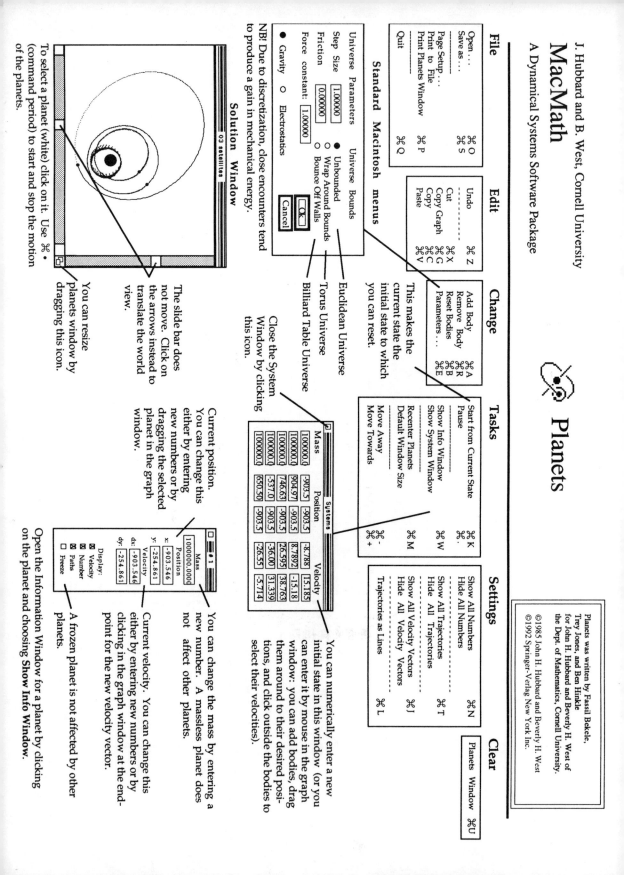

Planets

Planets was written by Fassil Bekele, Trey Jones, and Ben Hinkle for John H. Hubbard and Beverly H. West of the Dept. of Mathematics, Cornell University.
©1985 John H. Hubbard and Beverly H. West
©1992 Springer-Verlag New York Inc.

File

Open... ⌘O
Save as... ⌘S
Page Setup...
Print to File
Print Planets Window ⌘P
Quit ⌘Q

Edit

Undo ⌘Z
Cut ⌘X
Copy Graph ⌘G
Copy ⌘C
Paste ⌘V

Standard Macintosh menus

Change

Add Body ⌘A
Remove Body ⌘R
Reset Bodies ⌘B
Parameters... ⌘E

This makes the current state the initial state to which you can reset.

Tasks

Start from Current State ⌘K
Pause ⌘.
Show Info Window ⌘W
Show System Window
Recenter Planets ⌘M
Default Window Size
Move Away ⌘-
Move Towards ⌘+

Settings

Show All Numbers ⌘N
Hide All Numbers
Show All Trajectories ⌘T
Hide All Trajectories
Show All Velocity Vectors ⌘J
Hide All Velocity Vectors
Trajectories as Lines ⌘L

Clear

Planets Window ⌘U

Universe Parameters

Step Size 1.00000
Friction 0.00000
Force constant: 1.00000

● Gravity   ○ Electrostatics

Universe Bounds
● Unbounded
○ Wrap Around Bounds
○ Bounce Off Walls

OK   Cancel

Euclidean Universe
Torus Universe
Billiard Table Universe

Close the System Window by clicking this icon.

Solution Window
03 satellites

NB! Due to discretization, close encounters tend to produce a gain in mechanical energy.

To select a planet (white) click on it. Use ⌘ · (command period) to start and stop the motion of the planets.

You can resize planets window by dragging this icon.

The slide bar does not move. Click on the arrows instead to translate the world view.

You can change this either by entering new numbers or by dragging the selected planet in the graph window.

Mass	Position		Velocity	
100000.0	-903.5	-903.5	-8.788	15.185
100000.0	904.97	-903.5	8.7892	-15.18
100000.0	746.63	-903.5	26.595	38.763
100000.0	-537.0	26.595	-36.00	-15.18
650.50	-903.5	-36.00	26.55	31.339
100000.0	-903.5	-26.55	-26.55	-5.714

Systems

□ #1
Mass 1000000.000
Position   x: -903.546   y: -254.861
Velocity   dx: -903.546   dy: -254.861
Display: ☒ Velocity ☒ Number ☒ Paths ☐ Freeze

Current position. You can change this either by entering new numbers or by dragging the selected planet in the graph window.

Current velocity. You can change this either by entering new numbers or by clicking in the graph window at the end-point for the new velocity vector.

You can change the mass by entering a new number. A massless planet does not affect other planets.

A frozen planet is not affected by other planets.

Open the Information Window for a planet by clicking on the planet and choosing Show Info Window.

You can numerically enter a new initial state in this window (or you can enter it by mouse in the graph window: you can add bodies, drag them around to their desired positions, and click outside the bodies to select their velocities).